ANTON CHEKHOV 1860. His first ambi doctor, although his p pay for his education nancial aid for his stu while pursuing his professional goal began to develop an interest in writing. Ultimately, his interest in literature overtook his dedication to medicine and he fully committed himself to a literary career. THE CHERRY ORCHARD, like THE THREE SISTERS, which also appears in the Avon Library, was produced under the great Russian director, Stanislavski, in a Moscow Art Theater performance. THE CHERRY ORCHARD portrays the twisted world of emotional paradox, contradictory behavior and environmental oppressions. Perhaps his best-known play, THE CHERRY ORCHARD is an example of Chekhov's unique and enduring contribution to the literature of the theater. He died in 1904, the year THE CHERRY ORCHARD was written.

HENRY POPKIN serves as drama critic of *Vogue*, reviews New York theater for the London *Times*, and has contributed to the New York *Herald Tribune*, *The New York Times*, *Kenyon Review*, *Sewanee Review*, *Commentary*, *Tulane Drama Review*, *New Republic*, *New Leader* and other periodicals. He has recently edited *New British Drama*, a revised edition of Barrett H. Clark's *European Theories of the Drama*, and *The Concise Encyclopedia of Modern Drama*.

Plays in The Avon Library

Tom Jones and Harvey Schmidt
THE FANTASTICKS
W121 $1.25

Anton Chekhov
THE THREE SISTERS
GS5 50¢

George Bernard Shaw
ARMS AND THE MAN
GS13 50¢

Henrik Ibsen
GHOSTS
GS8 50¢
THE WILD DUCK
GS3 50¢

John Millington Synge
THE PLAYBOY OF THE WESTERN WORLD
GS12 50¢

August Strindberg
MISS JULIE
GS9 50¢

Oscar Wilde
THE IMPORTANCE OF BEING EARNEST
GS4 50¢

Anton Chekhov

The Cherry Orchard

AN AUTHORITATIVE TEXT EDITION

Translated by Avrahm Yarmolinsky

Critical Material Selected and
Introduced by Henry Popkin

The Avon Theater Library

AVON BOOKS
A division of
The Hearst Corporation
959 Eighth Avenue
New York, N. Y. 10019

First Printing (Avon Theater Library), December, 1965

Second Printing, April, 1968

Cover illustration by Saul Lambert

Printed in the U.S.A.

ACKNOWLEDGMENTS

The Cherry Orchard by Anton Chekhov, translated by Avrahm
Yarmolinsky, from *The Portable Chekhov,* translated by Avrahm
Yarmolinsky, Copyright 1947 by The Viking Press, Inc., re-
printed by permission of The Viking Press.

Material from *The Oxford Chekhov,* Volume III, edited and
translated by Ronald Hingley. © Ronald Hingley 1964. Re-
printed by permission of Oxford University Press.

Contents

INTRODUCTION

INTRODUCTION

Sixty years after his death, no modern dramatist is more alive than Chekhov. Everywhere his plays are being restaged, and now· he must be said to share with Bernard Shaw the distinction of being that founder of the modern drama whose work is most often performed. Indeed, in the world theater, the revivals of his four major plays—*The Sea Gull, Uncle Vanya, The Three Sisters,* and *The Cherry Orchard*—surely outnumber the productions of any four plays by Shaw. For vitality on the contemporary stage, he has left Ibsen and Strindberg far behind, and, in comparison, Hauptmann is no more than a textbook name.

One symptom of Chekhov's extraordinary appeal is the interest that some dramatists have taken in rewriting his plays. The efforts of these writers testify to the interest and the universality of Chekhov's work; their failure reminds us of its uniqueness, its direct dependence upon the time and place in which and concerning which it was written: Tsarist Russia at the turn of the century. It will be useful to look at some of the Chekhov adaptations in order to see where they go wrong and, thus, to isolate the ineffable and irreplaceable Chekhov quality.

Several years ago, the American director Joshua Logan rewrote *The Cherry Orchard* as *The Wisteria Trees,* moving Chekhov's characters from Russia to Louisiana of the same period. The freed serfs became freed Negro slaves—all except the Louisiana equivalent of Lopahin, represented as a redneck who had risen in the world. Helen Hayes, who played the Ranevskaya of the postbellum South, told the press that she had long been looking forward to playing Chekhov's heroine. She would have been well advised to pursue her original ambition, since Chekhov's play gained nothing and lost much by being transplanted. The characters were too Russian to be easily Americanized. Russian lethargy was out of place in a setting that required some signs of American energy, and so Logan found that he had to supply new motivation for the characters' fecklessness. He accomplished this end by furnishing two of them with new elements of unrequited love. It should be added that *The Wisteria Trees* came at a time when Chekhov's plays were no longer getting major professional productions in the United States. Odd notions prevailed concerning the gloom and even the difficulty of Chekhov's plays. The argument for *The Wisteria Trees* was that the adaptation constituted the only palatable form in which a dose of Chekhov could be administered to the American public. Its failure seemed to be a convincing demonstration that no one wanted Chekhov in any form. Broadway was not to see another Chekhov play for more than a dozen years.

If Logan offered a Chekhov-substitute for those who were not permitted to sample the genuine article, another one of the Chekhov-adapters furnished a Chekhov-companion on the assumption that allusions to Chekhov would be familiar to an audience fortunate enough to know the original. He was the leading Rumanian dramatist, Horia Lovinescu, who a few years ago rewrote *The Three Sisters* as *The Boga Sisters*. His heroines were three Rumanian sisters whose history he traced during the war and in the years immediately following. His peculiar innovation was to introduce some rather heavy-handed poetic justice. The oldest sister, who works hardest (in Lovinescu, as in Chekhov) and who never comes close to any hint of romance in Chekhov, gets her man in Lovinescu's play—and a political commissar at that. The second, who is, in Chekhov, married to an industrious but boring schoolmaster and has a love affair with a military officer, is rebuked by Lovinescu as a flirtatious, wasteful parasite; the virtuous schoolmaster, on the other hand, is martyred by a counterrevolutionary. Lovinescu's third sister, like Chekhov's, intends to marry a young aristocrat who, as in Chekhov, is shot. There the re-semblance ends; Lovinescu's aristocrat richly deserves his fate because, true to his inheritance, he is a foe of the revolutionary regime. Lovinescu has lost sight of the characters' particular and specific humanity and the de-mands it makes upon our compassion. Chekhov always makes sure that his characters' folly is fully explained and understood; he creates no villains and never induces his audience to expect or desire any punishment to befall the frail, unhappy creatures on the stage. Natasha and Solyony in *The Three Sisters* come as close as any of Chekhov's characters to being true-bred villains, but even their hostilities and their vindictiveness are so fully interpreted that they can be viewed as symptoms of a spiritual ailment. Giving marks for good or bad conduct, handing out rewards and punishments, as, in effect, Lovinescu does, is foreign to Chekhov's design. In these remarkably impersonal plays, one quality of the author's is clearly visible. It is his tenderness towards all his creations, his gentle, humorous but feeling sympathy with all of them. He does not *want* to punish them, and, happily, he knows that life does not punish or reward in any intelligible fashion; things simply happen, and the dramatist's proper function, admirably understood by Chekhov, is to make them happen naturally.

Why rewrite Chekhov? I suppose that to rewrite Chekhov is to pay him a compliment. Logan and Lovi-nescu, approaching the plays with very different inten-tions, were both so impressed with the reality of Chek-hov's characters that they wanted to claim them as their own and to revise and reorder their disorderly lives for them. What they failed to recognize is that these lives, as Chekhov conceived them, in all their disorder and confusion, are as right and inevitable as the vivid per-sonal qualities that so attract the rewriters.

Only in the English-speaking world is Chekhov's emergence as a popular dramatist new or surprising. Of course, he has long been a classic in his native Russia, and, naturally enough, when the Moscow Art Theater, with which Chekhov has always been identified, visited

New York, two of the four plays it brought were by
Chekhov. Paris gets a new Chekhov play nearly every
year from the Pitoeff family, which virtually holds a
monopoly upon Parisian productions of Chekhov; but,
a few years ago, the august and conservative Comédie
Française added *Uncle Vanya* to its repertoire. In London, one of the first plays staged at the newly founded
National Theater was *Uncle Vanya,* which proved to be,
by a considerable margin, the most popular and the most
widely admired production in the first year of this new
theater's life. The United States has lately rediscovered
Chekhov by way of its repertory theaters. *The Three
Sisters* was the principal success with both critics and
public in the first year of the Tyrone Guthrie Theater of
Minneapolis. The subsequent production of the same
play by the Actors Studio of New York was more con-
troversial, but the Studio thought well enough of its work
to take *The Three Sisters* to London, where it received
a phenomenally unfavorable reception; some critics were
even moved to say that, regretfully and unwillingly, they
had begun to wonder if Chekhov was really a great
dramatist. Perhaps we should be grateful for their regret
and their unwillingness, but we may also thank them
for stumbling onto an important fact. More than most
dramatists, Chekhov requires to be properly acted. It is
true that no dramatist is foolproof. Shakespeare's plays
can be bungled as easily as any others, but bad versions
of Chekhov create remarkably unpleasant effects of lu-
gubriousness and inertia; they foster a popular and ma-
licious caricature of Chekhov that has long prevailed in
America. The long American neglect of Chekhov derived from this caricature, from the suspicion of total
inaction, of a pervasive and peculiarly Russian gloom,
or characters stumbling around ignoring each other, ad-
dressing their bitter complaints to convenient doors and
windows, calling one another by indistinguishable three-
barreled Russian names, forever attempting to shoot
themselves and forever missing. (One authoritative
newspaper recently had a careless reference to Uncle
Vanya's trying to shoot himself and missing. Actually,

Vanya tries to shoot someone else and misses. It is Treplev in *The Sea Gull* who botches his own suicide, not by missing himself, but by inflicting a wound that is not fatal.) An inept but characteristic American parody of *The Cherry Orchard* parts the young couple, Trofimov and Anya, at the end, as Chekhov does; when the logic of this parting is questioned, someone explains "That's Chekhov" and then hastily corrects the remark to "That's life." By introducing new motivation for Chekhov's characters, Joshua Logan, in *The Wisteria Trees,* showed some of the same incomprehension of Chekhov's purposes.

Are Chekhov's people really so oddly inactive, so feckless, so dead? Are they all possessed of a morbidity that permits no rational explanation? For the most part, the opposite is true. Chekhov's characters are extremely steadfast in fighting off an entirely justifiable morbidity. Chekhov, in his stories, as in his plays, was especially attentive to the plight of sensitive, cultured people who are compelled to live out their lives in the dreary miasma of the Russian provinces. To do their jobs, to continue to live and to suffer, to run an estate (as Vanya does) or to teach school (as two of the three sisters do) in such an environment is not to be inactive or feckless but to be very brave. Still, it must be conceded that a certain inaction and some consequent gloom pervade three of Chekhov's major plays—*Uncle Vanya, The Three Sisters,* and *The Cherry Orchard.* (*The Sea Gull* has more external action and more obviously "dramatic" events, but even this play was so different that its first performance was a disaster in St. Petersburg.) There is, normally, very little excitement in the lives of Vanya and his equally frustrated fellow-intellectual, in the lives of the Moscow-bred sisters who are doomed to dwell in the provinces, or in the lives of the effete proprietors of the celebrated orchard. If Chekhov left matters there, if he confined himself to merely depicting these wretched folk, the popular misapprehension of him would have some basis. But what he has done is to create a dramatic context that sets off the native lethargy of these charac-

ters. For the brief, highly selected period of the action
in each play, he has chosen to examine them at what
may be the only exciting and eventful moments of their
lives. These people do not themselves create excitement;
they do not challenge the universe. Their destiny, perhaps even their preference, may be to do nothing at all,
but, once in a lifetime, the world moves in upon them.
Action overtakes them in spite of themselves, and that is
the subject of the play. The effect may be either tragic
or comic or both at once when these people hear the
world's call to arms and find, with the best will in the
world, that they have lost the habit, the capacity, or the
taste for action. But to create comic and tragic compart-
ments is to misinterpret Chekhov. The events that occur
in his plays are at one and the same time tragic and
comic, pathetic and ridiculous, hopeless and hopeful.
Chekhov's great virtue is always to recognize that life is
not all one thing or the other, that any interesting and
significant human experience is too complex to permit
easy interpretations or simple responses.

Life, in these plays, suddenly catches up with people
whom it has previously passed by. Having lost the habit
of actively pursuing practical goals, having forgotten how
to make decisions and meet challenges, they are abruptly
confronted with an opportunity to act. This brief encounter with reality sets up the tensions that dominate
the play, tensions between a lifetime of inertia and a
moment of action. Consider Uncle Vanya, whose labori-
ous, lonely existence is suddenly interrupted by two
challenges: the threatened loss of his lifelong work and
a proffered invitation to romance. He meets one challenge as lamely as he does the other. Too furious and too
startled to conduct a rational argument, he tries to
shoot the brother-in-law who wants to rob him of the
estate; his efforts at a flirtation with his tormentor's wife
are equally inept and equally fruitless. Is he lethargic or
paralyzed? All the rest of his life, perhaps he is. He may
be spiritually motionless, except for self-pity, for decades
previous and decades to come, but Chekhov takes the
trouble to catch him at the only moment that illuminates

both the tragedy and the comedy of his life. In *Uncle Vanya,* it is much the same with Astrov, but his life is not quite so deeply buried as Vanya's, and so he is less deeply affected by the crisis of the play. Astrov is a relatively serious person, but Vanya is somehow a figure of fun. Perhaps no one in Chekhov is quite so comic as Vanya firing at close range at his arch-enemy, the Philistine professor, and missing him, but no one is so tragic, either. Missing at close range is always good for laughs, and Chekhov unquestionably knew how to wring laughter out of outlandish actions, funny lines, and even meaningful pauses, but the real comedy and the real pathos, too, derive, as everywhere in Chekhov, from character. The real point is that Vanya is an intellectual, a man of thought, and that he, of all men, has no business turning imbecile and trying to shoot people.

The lives of Chekhov's three sisters have been dull enough before the few years of the play's action. Like Vanya and Astrov and like many wretched souls in Chekhov's stories, they are bright, interesting, cultivated individuals who have the misfortune to live in a dismal cultural desert. Once more, Chekhov has deliberately chosen the one brief moment when hopes flare up and when some escape or at least some relief seems possible, and then, finally, the military officers whose company has made life bearable are all assigned elsewhere. Every hope turns out badly. No doubt responding to the imminence of their coming departure, two officers propose marriage to the youngest sister; the one she rejects shoots the one she accepts, effectively cutting off her escape. The middle sister has an affair with a married officer who must march off with the rest at the end. But, even here, in a play that Chekhov chose to call a drama and not a comedy, his intention is not to present unrelieved gloom. In fact, at the time of the original production, the play's comic elements induced its director, Konstantin Stanislavsky, to misjudge its qualities and to take it for a comedy.

Chekhov's work is full of contradictions, but then, so is life itself. Is he tragic or comic? Is life tragic or comic? The answer to that hard question depends on where you are standing. Vanya is tragic to himself and sometimes to us, but, sometimes, when he is taking himself most seriously, he is most ludicrous to us. The three sisters' bad-tempered sister-in-law is never so ridiculous as when she stands upon her dignity. *The Cherry Orchard* is the most comic of the major plays, the only one that Chekhov completed, as he said, without a pistol shot, but it concerns the irreparable loss of something beautiful and the end of an ancient family. Chekhov manages, at the same time, to make us feel the loss and still see the humor of the situation.

Was Chekhov an optimist or a pessimist, a liberal or a conservative? Again, one question must be answered with another: Is life liberal or conservative? The plays give contradictory evidence. Chekhov helps to explain the contradictions in a letter of 1889:

I am afraid of those who look for a tendency between the lines, and who are determined to regard me either as a liberal or as a conservative. I am not a liberal, not a conservative, not a believer in gradual progress, not a monk, not an indifferentist. I should like to be a free artist and nothing more . . .

On the other hand, he wrote in his Notebook:

Really decent people are only to be found amongst men who have definite either conservative or radical convictions; so-called moderate men are much inclined to rewards, commissions, orders, promotions.

His characters complete no actions, and they make no progress. They are consoled only by the thought of some future happiness in which they cannot share and which they do not seem even to be in any way promoting. It must have been this evidence of pessimism that persuaded Lovinescu to rewrite him and create a more optimistic and "positive" version of *The Three Sisters*. Still, Chekhov kept inserting into his plays hopeful state-

ments about the future, spoken by idealistic characters
who themselves do little to bring about mankind's happier destiny—like Vershinin in *The Three Sisters* and
Trofimov in *The Cherry Orchard.* (The "hopeful"
spokesman of *Uncle Vanya,* Astrov, is more industrious,
but his flirtation with Yelena discloses a residue of
triviality in his character.) On the basis of such sentiments, the Soviet Union has apotheosized Chekhov and
hailed him as the prophet of the Russian Revolution.
Even now, even when the Moscow Art Theater tries to
"characterize" Trofimov, to make him a fallible, sometimes comic human being, it may be observed that the
other characters "freeze" and listen attentively, as they
do to no one else, whenever Trofimov launches one of
his optimistic, "progressive" perorations. Chekhov kept
a balance in his plays by emphasizing the personal
futility and absurdity of such idealists as Trofimov. In
his life, however, his progressive inclinations were more
evident; he drifted from an early alliance with a reac-
tionary publisher to a later concern with prison reform
and with establishing the innocence of Captain Dreyfus.

Chekhov's own life helps to explain his deep sympathy with the unfortunate. He was born January 17, 1860,
in Taganrog, near the Crimea. The son of an improvident grocer, he was brutally treated as a child, but, in
Moscow, at a remarkably early age, he became the
breadwinner of the family. By selling humorous stories,
he supported his parents, his brothers, and his sisters,
and he also put himself through medical school. He prac-
ticed medicine and continued to do so even when he was
earning substantial rewards as an author, more in order
to find material for his fiction than out of any sense of
dedication—or so he maintained. His early one-act
plays, like *The Bear* and *The Proposal,* were trivial,
funny sketches, in the mood of his stories of the same
period. The first full-length plays that he entrusted to
the world—an earlier play exists only in an untitled
manuscript—were both performed in 1889. *Ivanov,* a
tragedy of flagging idealism, was well received, but *The
Wood Demon,* about a fanatical exponent of reforesta-

tion, was not. His work took a more serious turn after the journey he undertook in 1890 to study prison conditions on the Siberian island of Sakhalin.

Following the failure of *The Sea Gull* in St. Petersburg in 1896, the same play was revived, with tremendous success, by the youthful Moscow Art Theater in 1898. Understandably encouraged, Chekhov threw himself with new vigor into writing plays, turning *The Wood Demon* into *Uncle Vanya* for production by the Moscow Art Theater in 1899. Writing *The Three Sisters* cost him more time and effort, and when the Moscow Art Theater staged it in 1901, this complex play was less warmly received. Later that year, he married a member of the company, Olga Knipper, who had played Masha in *The Three Sisters* and was to be Madame Ranevskaya in *The Cherry Orchard*. Dying of tuberculosis, he traveled abroad for his health and was in Yalta, in the south of Russia, when *The Cherry Orchard* had its successful opening in Moscow in 1904. The dramatist died later that year, July 2, 1904, at Badenweiler, Germany.

The Cherry Orchard is foreshadowed by the story "A Visit to Friends," in which the narrator visits some impractical gentlefolk who are facing the loss of their estate; he is fond of them, but he cannot help them. He is, in certain respects, like Lopahin in the subsequent play, and some of the impoverished gentlefolk bear at least superficial resemblances to Madame Ranevskaya, Gayev, and Varya. In *The Cherry Orchard,* however, Chekhov began with similar characters but went on to create a more symbolic, more concentrated, and more immediate crisis for his country gentry—the threatened loss of the orchard of the title, a garden which, like the family that owns it, is ancient, famous, beautiful, diverting, and entirely useless. The orchard, formerly useful but now only decorative, is a perfect emblem of the family and, indeed, of the social class to which the family belongs. Madame Ranevskaya and Gayev have outlived their moment in history, for the abolition of serfdom some forty years earlier has destroyed the feudal basis of the aristocracy and created the middle class that will take its place. Chekhov uses a non-realistic device to make us aware that an era is passing, that we are at a turning point in history: once during the action and again at the very end of the play, we hear a strange sound that cannot be satisfactorily explained—the same sound that was heard years before when serfdom was abolished.

We are at the same time aware of the inexorable pattern of history and of individual departures from this pattern. Instead of being at each other's throats, the gentlefolk and the bourgeois of the play are extremely friendly, in accordance with Chekhov's well-established preference for good-natured people. If *The Three Sisters* has its vindictive Natasha and its quarrelsome Solyony and *Uncle Vanya* its self-centered Serebryakov, *The Cherry Orchard* has no villain more serious than the rascally servant Yasha; that is to say, it has no villain other than the relentless course of events. Madame Ranevskaya and Gayev prove to be unwittingly attuned to history when they show themselves to be helpless and capable only of alternating between inertia and harebrained schemes, like hoping for some money from a rich aunt or for a rich husband for Anya. Lopahin, on the other hand, tries not to fulfill the historical function of his class. He does his best to save the estate for the aristocrats, but he makes it clear that, in order to save themselves, they must become bourgeoisie: they must hack down their heavily symbolic cherry orchard and go into business. Naturally, they will not listen to good advice, Lopahin is compelled to buy the estate (which the old owners cannot save in any case, Gayev having been forced out of the bidding at an early stage), and he permits himself one brief moment of playing his natural, instinctive role as a bourgeois, when, at the end of the third act, he glories in his success. Even after this event, the class-enemies continue to be friends. With characteristic good humor and light-headedness, the displaced owners of the orchard persuade themselves that the disaster that they feared so long was not really a calamity after all. They leave with few regrets and no resentment. Typically, they are too giddy to remember that they have left their old servant in the house, and Lopahin is too intent on business to propose marriage to Varya. No obligation—historical, economic, or even humane—can prevent Chekhov's characters from being simply themselves.

The student Trofimov speaks hopefully of the future and of a different life that will replace the present ascendancy of the bourgeoisie. While we may note that Chekhov, in a general way, shared Trofimov's optimism, we must also observe that this perennial student is a comic figure in a play that Chekhov called "a comedy, almost a farce." The dramatist has undermined Trofimov's oratory by making him an impractical visionary with an unsightly, scraggly beard, little grace, and no experience of love. He preaches to Madame Ranevskaya; when she insults him in return, he makes a dignified departure, ruins it by coming back with an afterthought, and then falls downstairs. If he is Chekhov's spokesman, he is a very special kind of spokesman, and the truths he expresses are no more infallible than the frail human vessel who utters them. In Chekhov, even the boldest optimistic generalizations are qualified by the ironic atmosphere that pervades the universe.

Henry Popkin

NOTE: Since the Russian alphabet is different from ours, inevitable differences in transliteration occur. The dramatist's name may be set down as Chekhov, Chekov, or Tchekhov, and one of his characters may be variously identified as Lopahin or Lopakhin. Although some variant transliterations have been preserved in the appendices, the names in question should still be readily identifiable.

The Cherry Orchard
by Anton Chekhov

Translated by Avrahm Yarmolinsky

A COMEDY IN FOUR ACTS

LIST OF CHARACTERS

Lubov Andreyevna Ranevskaya, a landowner
Anya, her seventeen-year-old daughter
Varya, her adopted daughter, twenty-two years old
Leonid Andreyevich Gayev, Mme. Ranevskaya's brother
Yermolay Alexeyevich Lopahin, a merchant
Pyotr Sergeyevich Trofimov, a student
Simeonov-Pishchik, a landowner
Charlotta Ivanovna, a governess
Semyon Yepihodov, a clerk
Dunyasha, a maid
Firs (pronounced *fierce*), a manservant, aged eighty-seven
Yasha, a young valet
A Tramp
Stationmaster, Post Office Clerk, Guests, Servants

The action takes place on Mme. Ranevskaya's estate.

ACT ONE

A room that is still called the nursery. One of the doors leads into ANYA's *room. Dawn, the sun will soon rise. It is May, the cherry trees are in blossom, but it is cold in the orchard; there is a morning frost. The windows are shut. Enter* DUNYASHA *with a candle, and* LOPAHIN *with a book in his hand.*

Lopahin.
The train is in, thank God. What time is it?

Dunyasha.
Nearly two. (*Puts out the candle.*) It's light already.

Lopahin.
How late is the train, anyway? Two hours at least. (*Yawns and stretches.*) I'm a fine one! What a fool I've made of myself! I came here on purpose to meet them at the station, and then I went and overslept. I fell asleep in my chair. How annoying! You might have waked me . . .

Dunyasha.
I thought you'd left. (*Listens.*) I think they're coming!

Lopahin.
(*Listens.*) No, they've got to get the luggage, and one thing and another . . . (*Pause.*) Lubov Andreyevna spent five years abroad, I don't know what she's like now. . . . She's a fine person—lighthearted, simple. I remember when I was a boy of fifteen, my poor father

—he had a shop here in the village then—punched me in the face with his fist and made my nose bleed. We'd come into the yard, I don't know what for, and he'd had a drop too much. Lubov Andreyevna, I remember her as if it were yesterday—she was still young and so slim—led me to the washbasin, in this very room ... in the nursery. "Don't cry, little peasant," she said, "it'll heal in time for your wedding ..." (*Pause.*) Little peasant ... my father was a peasant, it's true, and here I am in a white waistcoat and yellow shoes. A pig in a pastry shop, you might say. It's true I'm rich, I've got a lot of money. ... But when you look at it closely, I'm a peasant through and through. (*Pages the book.*) Here I've been reading this book and I didn't understand a word of it. ... I was reading it and fell asleep ... (*Pause.*)

Dunyasha.
And the dogs were awake all night, they feel that their masters are coming.

Lopahin.
Dunyasha, why are you so—

Dunyasha.
My hands are trembling. I'm going to faint.

Lopahin.
You're too soft, Dunyasha. You dress like a lady, and look at the way you do your hair. That's not right. One should remember one's place.

(*Enter* YEPIHODOV *with a bouquet; he wears a jacket and highly polished boots that squeak badly. He drops the bouquet as he comes in.*)

Yepihodov.
(*Picking up the bouquet.*) Here, the gardener sent these, said you're to put them in the dining room. (*Hands the bouquet to* DUNYASHA.)

Lopahin.
And bring me some *kvass*.

Dunyasha.
Yes, sir. (*Exits.*)

Yepihodov.
There's a frost this morning—three degrees below—

and yet the cherries are all in blossom. I cannot approve of our climate. (*Sighs.*) I cannot. Our climate does not activate properly. And, Yermolay Alexeyevich, allow me to make a further remark. The other day I bought myself a pair of boots, and I make bold to assure you, they squeak so that it is really intolerable. What should I grease them with?

Lopahin.
Oh, get out! I'm fed up with you.

Yepihodov.
Every day I meet with misfortune. And I don't complain, I've got used to it, I even smile.

(DUNYASHA *enters, hands* LOPAHIN *the kvass.*)

Yepihodov.
I am leaving. (*Stumbles against a chair, which falls over.*) There! (*Triumphantly, as it were.*) There again, you see what sort of circumstance, pardon the expression. . . . It is absolutely phenomenal! (*Exits.*)

Dunyasha.
You know, Yermolay Alexeyevich, I must tell you, Yepihodov has proposed to me.

Lopahin.
Ah!

Dunyasha.
I simply don't know . . . he's a quiet man, but sometimes when he starts talking, you can't make out what he means. He speaks nicely—and it's touching—but you can't understand it. I sort of like him though, and he is crazy about me. He's an unlucky man . . . every day something happens to him. They tease him about it here . . . they call him, Two-and-Twenty Troubles.

Lopahin.
(*Listening.*) There! I think they're coming.

Dunyasha.
They *are* coming! What's the matter with me? I feel cold all over.

Lopahin.
They really are coming. Let's go and meet them. Will

she recognize me? We haven't seen each other for
five years.

Dunyasha.

(*In a flutter.*) I'm going to faint this minute. . . . Oh,
I'm going to faint!

(*Two carriages are heard driving up to the house.*
LOPAHIN *and* DUNYASHA *go out quickly. The stage is
left empty. There is a noise in the adjoining rooms.*
FIRS, *who had driven to the station to meet* LUBOV
ANDREYEVNA RANEVSKAYA, *crosses the stage hurriedly,
leaning on a stick. He is wearing an old-fashioned
livery and a tall hat. He mutters to himself indistinctly.
The hubbub offstage increases. A* VOICE: "Come, let's
go this way." *Enter* LUBOV ANDREYEVNA, ANYA, *and*
CHARLOTTA IVANOVNA *with a pet dog on a leash, all in
traveling dresses;* VARYA, *wearing a coat and kerchief;*
GAYEV, SIMEONOV-PISHCHIK, LOPAHIN, DUNYASHA *with
a bag and an umbrella, servants with luggage. All walk
across the room.*)

Anya.

Let's go this way. Do you remember what room this
is, Mamma?

Mme. Ranevskaya.

(*Joyfully, through her tears.*) The nursery!

Varya.

How cold it is! My hands are numb. (*To* MME. RANEV-
SKAYA.) Your rooms are just the same as they were,
Mamma, the white one and the violet.

Mme. Ranevskaya.

The nursery! My darling, lovely room! I slept here
when I was a child . . . (*Cries.*) And here I am, like
a child again! (*Kisses her brother and* VARYA, *and
then her brother again.*) Varya's just the same as
ever, like a nun. And I recognized Dunyasha. (*Kisses*
DUNYASHA.)

Gayev.

The train was two hours late. What do you think of
that? What a way to manage things!

Charlotta.

(*To* PISHCHIK.) My dog eats nuts, too.

Pishchik.
(*In amazement.*) You don't say so!

(*All go out, except* ANYA *and* DUNYASHA.)

Dunyasha.
We've been waiting for you for hours. (*Takes* ANYA's *hat and coat.*)

Anya.
I didn't sleep on the train for four nights and now I'm frozen . . .

Dunyasha.
It was Lent when you left; there was snow and frost, and now . . . My darling! (*Laughs and kisses her.*) I have been waiting for you, my sweet, my darling! But I must tell you something . . . I can't put it off another minute . . .

Anya.
(*Listlessly.*) What now?

Dunyasha.
The clerk, Yepihodov, proposed to me, just after Easter.

Anya.
There you are, at it again . . . (*Straightening her hair.*) I've lost all my hairpins . . . (*She is staggering with exhaustion.*)

Dunyasha.
Really, I don't know what to think. He loves me—he loves me so!

Anya.
(*Looking toward the door of her room, tenderly.*) My own room, my windows, just as though I'd never been away. I'm home! Tomorrow morning I'll get up and run into the orchard. Oh, if I could only get some sleep. I didn't close my eyes during the whole journey —I was so anxious.

Dunyasha.
Pyotr Sergeyevich came the day before yesterday.

Anya.
(*Joyfully.*) Petya!

Dunyasha.
He's asleep in the bathhouse. He has settled there. He said he was afraid of being in the way. (*Looks*

at her watch.) I should wake him, but Miss Varya told me not to. "Don't you wake him," she said.

(*Enter* VARYA *with a bunch of keys at her belt.*)

Varya.
Dunyasha, coffee, and be quick. . . . Mamma's asking for coffee.

Dunyasha.
In a minute. (*Exits.*)

Varya.
Well, thank God, you've come. You're home again. (*Fondling* ANYA.) My darling is here again. My pretty one is back.

Anya.
Oh, what I've been through!

Varya.
I can imagine.

Anya.
When we left, it was Holy Week, it was cold then, and all the way Charlotta chattered and did her tricks. Why did you have to saddle me with Charlotta?

Varya.
You couldn't have traveled all alone, darling—at seventeen!

Anya.
We got to Paris, it was cold there, snowing. My French is dreadful. Mamma lived on the fifth floor; I went up there, and found all kinds of Frenchmen, ladies, an old priest with a book. The place was full of tobacco smoke, and so bleak. Suddenly I felt sorry for Mamma, so sorry, I took her head in my arms and hugged her and couldn't let go of her. Afterward Mamma kept fondling me and crying . . .

Varya.
(*Through tears.*) Don't speak of it . . . don't.

Anya.
She had already sold her villa at Mentone, she had nothing left, nothing. I hadn't a kopeck left either, we had only just enough to get home. And Mamma wouldn't understand! When we had dinner at the stations, she always ordered the most expensive dishes, and tipped the waiters a whole ruble. Charlotta, too.

And Yasha kept ordering, too—it was simply awful. You know Yasha's Mamma's footman now, we brought him here with us.

Varya.
Yes, I've seen the blackguard.

Anya.
Well, tell me—have you paid the interest?

Varya.
How could we?

Anya.
Good heavens, good heavens!

Varya.
In August the estate will be put up for sale.

Anya.
My God!

Lopahin.
(*Peeps in at the door and bleats.*) Meh-h-h. (*Disappears.*)

Varya.
(*Through tears.*) What I couldn't do to him! (*Shakes her fist threateningly.*)

Anya.
(*Embracing* VARYA, *gently.*) Varya, has he proposed to you? (VARYA *shakes her head.*) But he loves you. Why don't you come to an understanding? What are you waiting for?

Varya.
Oh, I don't think anything will ever come of it. He's too busy, he has no time for me . . . pays no attention to me. I've washed my hands of him—I can't bear the sight of him. They all talk about our getting married, they all congratulate me—and all the time there's really nothing to it—it's all like a dream. (*In another tone.*) You have a new brooch—like a bee.

Anya.
(*Sadly.*) Mamma bought it. (*She goes into her own room and speaks gaily like a child.*) And you know, in Paris I went up in a balloon.

Varya.
My darling's home, my pretty one is back! (DUNYASHA *returns with the coffeepot and prepares coffee.* VARYA *stands at the door of* ANYA's *room.*) All day long,

darling, as I go about the house, I keep dreaming. If only we could marry you off to a rich man, I should feel at ease. Then I would go into a convent, and afterward to Kiev, to Moscow ... I would spend my life going from one holy place to another ... I'd go on and on. ... What a blessing that would be!

Anya.
The birds are singing in the orchard. What time is it?

Varya.
It must be after two. Time you were asleep, darling. (*Goes into* ANYA's *room.*) What a blessing that would be!

(YASHA *enters with a plaid and a traveling bag, crosses the stage.*)

Yasha.
(*Finically.*) May I pass this way, please?

Dunyasha.
A person could hardly recognize you, Yasha. Your stay abroad has certainly done wonders for you.

Yasha.
Hm-m ... and who are you?

Dunyasha.
When you went away I was that high—(*Indicating with her hand.*) I'm Dunyasha—Fyodor Kozoyedev's daughter. Don't you remember?

Yasha.
Hm! What a peach! (*He looks round and embraces her. She cries out and drops a saucer.* YASHA *leaves quickly.*)

Varya.
(*In the doorway, in a tone of annoyance.*) What's going on here?

Dunyasha.
(*Through tears.*) I've broken a saucer.

Varya.
Well, that's good luck.

Anya.
(*Coming out of her room.*) We ought to warn Mamma that Petya's here.

Varya.
I left orders not to wake him.

Anya.

(*Musingly.*) Six years ago father died. A month later brother Grisha was drowned in the river.... Such a pretty little boy he was—only seven. It was more than Mamma could bear, so she went away, went away without looking back ... (*Shudders.*) How well I understand her, if she only knew! (*Pauses.*) And Petya Trofimov was Grisha's tutor, he may remind her of it all ...

(*Enter* FIRS, *wearing a jacket and a white waistcoat. He goes up to the coffeepot.*)

Firs.

(*Anxiously.*) The mistress will have her coffee here. (*Puts on white gloves.*) Is the coffee ready? (*Sternly, to* DUNYASHA.) Here, you! And where's the cream?

Dunyasha.

Oh, my God! (*Exits quickly.*)

Firs.

(*Fussing over the coffeepot.*) Hah! the addlehead! (*Mutters to himself.*) Home from Paris. And the old master used to go to Paris too ... by carriage. (*Laughs.*)

Varya.

What is it, Firs?

Firs.

What is your pleasure, Miss? (*Joyfully.*) My mistress has come home, and I've seen her at last! Now I can die. (*Weeps with joy.*)

(*Enter* MME. RANEVSKAYA, GAYEV, *and* SIMEONOV-PISHCHIK. *The latter is wearing a tight-waisted, pleated coat of fine cloth, and full trousers.* GAYEV, *as he comes in, goes through the motions of a billiard player with his arms and body.*)

Mme. Ranevskaya.

Let's see, how does it go? Yellow ball in the corner! Bank shot in the side pocket!

Gayev.

I'll tip it in the corner! There was a time, Sister, when

you and I used to sleep in this very room and now I'm
fifty-one, strange as it may seem.

Lopahin.
Yes, time flies.

Gayev.
Who?

Lopahin.
I say, time flies.

Gayev.
It smells of patchouli here.

Anya.
I'm going to bed. Good night, Mamma. (*Kisses her
mother.*)

Mme. Ranevskaya.
My darling child! (*Kisses her hands.*) Are you happy
to be home? I can't come to my senses.

Anya.
Good night, Uncle.

Gayev.
(*Kissing her face and hands.*) God bless you, how like
your mother you are! (*To his sister.*) At her age,
Luba, you were just like her.

(ANYA *shakes hands with* LOPAHIN *and* PISHCHIK,
then goes out, shutting the door behind her.)

Mme. Ranevskaya.
She's very tired.

Pishchik.
Well, it was a long journey.

Varya.
(*To* LOPAHIN *and* PISHCHIK.) How about it, gentlemen? It's past two o'clock—isn't it time for you to go?

Mme. Ranevskaya.
(*Laughs.*) You're just the same as ever, Varya.
(*Draws her close and kisses her.*) I'll have my coffee
and then we'll all go. (FIRS *puts a small cushion under
her feet.*) Thank you, my dear. I've got used to coffee.
I drink it day and night. Thanks, my dear old man.
(*Kisses him.*)

Varya.
I'd better see if all the luggage has been brought in.
(*Exits.*)

Mme. Ranevskaya.
Can it really be I sitting here? (*Laughs.*) I feel like dancing, waving my arms about. (*Covers her face with her hands.*) But maybe I am dreaming! God knows I love my country, I love it tenderly; I couldn't look out of the window in the train, I kept crying so. (*Through tears.*) But I must have my coffee. Thank you, Firs, thank you, dear old man. I'm so happy that you're still alive.

Firs.
Day before yesterday.

Gayev.
He's hard of hearing.

Lopahin.
I must go soon, I'm leaving for Kharkov about five o'clock. How annoying! I'd like to have a good look at you, talk to you. . . . You're just as splendid as ever.

Pishchik.
(*Breathing heavily.*) She's even better-looking. . . . Dressed in the latest Paris fashion. . . . Perish my carriage and all its four wheels. . . .

Lopahin.
Your brother, Leonid Andreyevich, says I'm a vulgarian and an exploiter. But it's all the same to me—let him talk. I only want you to trust me as you used to. I want you to look at me with your touching, wonderful eyes, as you used to. Dear God! My father was a serf of your father's and grandfather's, but you, you yourself, did so much for me once . . . so much . . . that I've forgotten all about that; I love you as though you were my sister—even more.

Mme. Ranevskaya.
I can't sit still, I simply can't. (*Jumps up and walks about in violent agitation.*) This joy is too much for me. . . . Laugh at me, I'm silly! My own darling bookcase! My darling table! (*Kisses it.*)

Gayev.
While you were away, nurse died.

Mme. Ranevskaya.
(*Sits down and takes her coffee.*) Yes, God rest her soul; they wrote me about it.

Gayev.

And Anastasy is dead. Petrushka Kossoy has left me and has gone into town to work for the police inspector. (*Takes a box of sweets out of his pocket and begins to suck one.*)

Pishchik.

My daughter Dashenka sends her regards.

Lopahin.

I'd like to tell you something very pleasant—cheering. (*Glancing at his watch.*) I am leaving directly. There isn't much time to talk. But I will put it in a few words. As you know, your cherry orchard is to be sold to pay your debts. The sale is to be on the twenty-second of August; but don't you worry, my dear, you may sleep in peace; there is a way out. Here is my plan. Give me your attention! Your estate is only fifteen miles from the town; the railway runs close by it; and if the cherry orchard and the land along the riverbank were cut up into lots and these leased for summer cottages, you would have an income of at least 25,000 rubles a year out of it.

Gayev.

Excuse me.... What nonsense.

Mme. Ranevskaya.

I don't quite understand you, Yermolay Alexeyevich.

Lopahin.

You will get an annual rent of at least ten rubles per acre, and if you advertise at once, I'll give you any guarantee you like that you won't have a square foot of ground left by autumn, all the lots will be snapped up. In short, congratulations, you're saved. The location is splendid—by that deep river.... Only, of course, the ground must be cleared ... all the old buildings, for instance, must be torn down, and this house, too, which is useless, and, of course, the old cherry orchard must be cut down.

Mme. Ranevskaya.

Cut down? My dear, forgive me, but you don't know what you're talking about. If there's one thing that's interesting—indeed, remarkable—in the whole province, it's precisely our cherry orchard.

Lopahin.

The only remarkable thing about this orchard is that it's a very large one. There's a crop of cherries every other year, and you can't do anything with them; no one buys them.

Gayev.

This orchard is even mentioned in the encyclopedia.

Lopahin.

(*Glancing at his watch.*) If we can't think of a way out, if we don't come to a decision, on the twenty-second of August the cherry orchard and the whole estate will be sold at auction. Make up your minds! There's no other way out—I swear. None, none.

Firs.

In the old days, forty or fifty years ago, the cherries were dried, soaked, pickled, and made into jam, and we used to—

Gayev.

Keep still, Firs.

Firs.

And the dried cherries would be shipped by the cartload. It meant a lot of money! And in those days the dried cherries were soft and juicy, sweet, fragrant. . . . They knew the way to do it, then.

Mme. Ranevskaya.

And why don't they do it that way now?

Firs.

They've forgotten. Nobody remembers it.

Pishchik.

(*To* MME. RANEVSKAYA.) What's doing in Paris? Eh? Did you eat frogs there?

Mme. Ranevskaya.

I ate crocodiles.

Pishchik.

Just imagine!

Lopahin.

There used to be only landowners and peasants in the country, but now these summer people have appeared on the scene. . . . All the towns, even the small ones, are surrounded by these summer cottages; and in another twenty years, no doubt, the summer population will have grown enormously. Now the summer resident only drinks tea on his porch, but maybe he'll take to

working his acre, too, and then your cherry orchard
will be a rich, happy, luxuriant place.

Gayev.

(*Indignantly.*) Poppycock!

(*Enter* VARYA *and* YASHA.)

Varya.

There are two telegrams for you, Mamma dear. (*Picks
a key from the bunch at her belt and noisily opens an
old-fashioned bookcase.*) Here they are.

Mme. Ranevskaya.

They're from Paris. (*Tears them up without reading
them.*) I'm through with Paris.

Gayev.

Do you know, Luba, how old this bookcase is? Last
week I pulled out the bottom drawer and there I found
the date burnt in it. It was made exactly a hundred
years ago. Think of that! We could celebrate its cen-
tenary. True, it's an inanimate object, but nevertheless,
a bookcase . . .

Pishchik.

(*Amazed.*) A hundred years! Just imagine!

Gayev.

Yes. (*Tapping it.*) That's something. . . . Dear,
honored bookcase, hail to you who for more than a
century have served the glorious ideals of goodness
and justice! Your silent summons to fruitful toil has
never weakened in all those hundred years (*through
tears*), sustaining, through successive generations of
our family, courage and faith in a better future, and
fostering in us ideals of goodness and social consciousness. . . . (*Pauses.*)

Lopahin.

Yes . . .

Mme. Ranevskaya.

You haven't changed a bit, Leonid.

Gayev.

(*Somewhat embarrassed.*) I'll play it off the red in
the corner! Tip it in the side pocket!

Lopahin.

(*Looking at his watch.*) Well, it's time for me to
go . . .

Yasha.
(*Handing a pillbox to* MME. RANEVSKAYA.) Perhaps you'll take your pills now.

Pishchik.
One shouldn't take medicines, dearest lady, they do neither harm nor good. . . . Give them here, my valued friend. (*Takes the pillbox, pours the pills into his palm, blows on them, puts them in his mouth, and washes them down with some kvass.*) There!

Mme. Ranevskaya.
(*Frightened.*) You must be mad!

Pishchik.
I've taken all the pills.

Lopahin.
What a glutton!

(*All laugh.*)

Firs.
The gentleman visited us in Easter week, ate half a bucket of pickles, he did . . . (*Mumbles.*)

Mme. Ranevskaya.
What's he saying?

Varya.
He's been mumbling like that for the last three years—we're used to it.

Yasha.
His declining years!

(CHARLOTTA IVANOVNA, *very thin, tightly laced, dressed in white, a lorgnette at her waist, crosses the stage.*)

Lopahin.
Forgive me, Charlotta Ivanovna, I've not had time to greet you. (*Tries to kiss her hand.*)

Charlotta.
(*Pulling away her hand.*) If I let you kiss my hand, you'll be wanting to kiss my elbow next, and then my shoulder.

Lopahin.
I've no luck today. (*All laugh.*) Charlotta Ivanovna, show us a trick.

Mme. Ranevskaya.
Yes, Charlotta, do a trick for us.

Charlotta.
I don't see the need. I want to sleep. (*Exits.*)

Lopahin.
In three weeks we'll meet again. (*Kisses* MME.
RANEVSKAYA's *hand.*) Good-bye till then. Time's up.
(*To* GAYEV.) Bye-bye. (*Kisses* PISHCHIK.) Bye-bye.
(*Shakes hands with* VARYA, *then with* FIRS *and* YASHA.)
I hate to leave. (*To* MME. RANEVSKAYA.) If you make
up your mind about the cottages, let me know; I'll get
you a loan of 50,000 rubles. Think it over seriously.

Varya.
(*Crossly.*) Will you never go!

Lopahin.
I'm going, I'm going. (*Exits.*)

Gayev.
The vulgarian. But, excuse me . . . Varya's going to
marry him, he's Varya's fiancé.

Varya.
You talk too much, Uncle dear.

Mme. Ranevskaya.
Well, Varya, it would make me happy. He's a good
man.

Pishchik.
Yes, one must admit, he's a most estimable man. And
my Dashenka . . . she too says that . . . she says . . .
lots of things. (*Snores; but wakes up at once.*) All the
same, my valued friend, could you oblige me . . . with
a loan of 240 rubles? I must pay the interest on the
mortgage tomorrow.

Varya.
(*Alarmed.*) We can't, we can't!

Mme. Ranevskaya.
I really haven't any money.

Pishchik.
It'll turn up. (*Laughs.*) I never lose hope, I thought
everything was lost, that I was done for, when lo and
behold, the railway ran through my land . . . and I
was paid for it. . . . And something else will turn up
again, if not today, then tomorrow . . . Dashenka will
win two hundred thousand . . . she's got a lottery ticket.

Mme. Ranevskaya.
I've had my coffee, now let's go to bed.

Firs.

(*Brushes off* GAYEV; *admonishingly.*) You've got the wrong trousers on again. What am I to do with you?

Varya.

(*Softly.*) Anya's asleep. (*Gently opens the window.*) The sun's up now, it's not a bit cold. Look, Mamma dear, what wonderful trees. And heavens, what air! The starlings are singing!

Gayev.

(*Opens the other window.*) The orchard is all white. You've not forgotten it? Luba? That's the long alley that runs straight, straight as an arrow; how it shines on moonlight nights, do you remember? You've not forgotten?

Mme. Ranevskaya.

(*Looking out of the window into the orchard.*) Oh, my childhood, my innocent childhood. I used to sleep in this nursery—I used to look out into the orchard, happiness waked with me every morning, the orchard was just the same then . . . nothing has changed. (*Laughs with joy.*) All, all white! Oh, my orchard! After the dark, rainy autumn and the cold winter, you are young again, and full of happiness, the heavenly angels have not left you. . . . If I could free my chest and my shoulders from this rock that weighs on me, if I could only forget the past!

Gayev.

Yes, and the orchard will be sold to pay our debts, strange as it may seem. . . .

Mme. Ranevskaya.

Look! There is our poor mother walking in the orchard . . . all in white . . . (*Laughs with joy.*) It is she!

Gayev.

Where?

Varya.

What are you saying, Mamma dear!

Mme. Ranevskaya.

There's no one there, I just imagined it. To the right, where the path turns toward the arbor, there's a little white tree, leaning over, that looks like a woman . . .

(TROFIMOV *enters, wearing a shabby student's uni- form and spectacles.*)

Mme. Ranevskaya.
What an amazing orchard! White masses of blossom, the blue sky . . .

Trofimov.
Lubov Andreyevna! (*She looks round at him.*) I just want to pay my respects to you, then I'll leave at once. (*Kisses her hand ardently.*) I was told to wait until morning, but I hadn't the patience . . . (MME. RANEVSKAYA *looks at him, perplexed.*)

Varya.
(*Through tears.*) This is Petya Trofimov.

Trofimov.
Petya Trofimov, formerly your Grisha's tutor. . . . Can I have changed so much? (MME. RANEVSKAYA *em- braces him and weeps quietly.*)

Gayev.
(*Embarrassed.*) Don't, don't, Luba.

Varya.
(*Crying.*) I told you, Petya, to wait until tomorrow.

Mme. Ranevskaya.
My Grisha . . . my little boy . . . Grisha . . . my son.

Varya.
What can one do, Mamma dear, it's God's will.

Trofimov.
(*Softly, through tears.*) There . . . there.

Mme. Ranevskaya.
(*Weeping quietly.*) My little boy was lost . . . drowned. Why? Why, my friend? (*More quietly.*) Anya's asleep in there, and here I am talking so loudly . . . making all this noise. . . . But tell me, Petya, why do you look so badly? Why have you aged so?

Trofimov.
A mangy master, a peasant woman in the train called me.

Mme. Ranevskaya.
You were just a boy then, a dear little student, and now your hair's thin—and you're wearing glasses! Is it possible you're still a student? (*Goes toward the door.*)

Trofimov.
I suppose I'm a perpetual student.

Mme. Ranevskaya.
(*Kisses her brother, then* VARYA.) Now, go to bed. . . .
You have aged, too, Leonid.

Pishchik.
(*Follows her.*) So now we turn in. Oh, my gout! I'm
staying the night here . . . Lubov Andreyevna, my
angel, tomorrow morning . . . I do need 240 rubles.

Gayev.
He keeps at it.

Pishchik.
I'll pay it back, dear . . . it's a trifling sum.

Mme. Ranevskaya.
All right, Leonid will give it to you. Give it to him,
Leonid.

Gayev.
Me give it to him! That's a good one!

Mme. Ranevskaya.
It can't be helped. Give it to him! He needs it. He'll
pay it back.

(MME. RANEVSKAYA, TROFIMOV, PISHCHIK, *and* FIRS
go out; GAYEV, VARYA, *and* YASHA *remain.*)

Gayev.
Sister hasn't got out of the habit of throwing money
around. (*To* YASHA.) Go away, my good fellow, you
smell of the barnyard.

Yasha.
(*With a grin.*) And you, Leonid Andreyevich, are
just the same as ever.

Gayev.
Who? (*To* VARYA.) What did he say?

Varya.
(*To* YASHA.) Your mother's come from the village;
she's been sitting in the servants' room since yesterday,
waiting to see you.

Yasha.
Botheration!

Varya.
You should be ashamed of yourself!

Yasha.
She's all I needed! She could have come tomorrow.
(*Exits.*)

Varya.
Mamma is just the same as ever; she hasn't changed a bit. If she had her own way, she'd keep nothing for herself.

Gayev.
Yes . . . (*Pauses.*) If a great many remedies are offered for some disease, it means it is incurable; I keep thinking and racking my brains; I have many remedies, ever so many, and that really means none. It would be fine if we came in for a legacy; it would be fine if we married off our Anya to a very rich man; or we might go to Yaroslavl and try our luck with our aunt, the Countess. She's very, very rich, you know . . .

Varya.
(*Weeping.*) If only God would help us!

Gayev.
Stop bawling. Aunt's very rich, but she doesn't like us. In the first place, Sister married a lawyer who was no nobleman . . . (ANYA *appears in the doorway.*) She married beneath her, and it can't be said that her behavior has been very exemplary. She's good, kind, sweet, and I love her, but no matter what extenuating circumstances you may adduce, there's no denying that she has no morals. You sense it in her least gesture.

Varya.
(*In a whisper.*) Anya's in the doorway.

Gayev.
Who? (*Pauses.*) It's queer, something got into my right eye—my eyes are going back on me. . . . And on Thursday, when I was in the circuit court—

(*Enter* ANYA.)

Varya.
Why aren't you asleep, Anya?

Anya.
I can't get to sleep, I just can't.

Gayev.
My little pet! (*Kisses* ANYA's *face and hands.*) My child! (*Weeps.*) You are not my niece, you're my angel! You're everything to me. Believe me, believe—

Anya.
I believe you, Uncle. Everyone loves you and respects

you . . . but, Uncle dear, you must keep still. . . . You must. What were you saying just now about my mother? Your own sister? What made you say that?

Gayev.
Yes, yes . . . (*Covers his face with her hand.*) Really, that was awful! Good God! Heaven help me! Just now I made a speech to the bookcase . . . so stupid! And only after I was through, I saw how stupid it was.

Varya.
It's true, Uncle dear, you ought to keep still. Just don't talk, that's all.

Anya.
If you could only keep still, it would make things easier for you, too.

Gayev.
I'll keep still. (*Kisses* ANYA's *and* VARYA's *hands.*) I will. But now about business. On Thursday I was in court; well, there were a number of us there, and we began talking of one thing and another, and this and that, and do you know, I believe it will be possible to raise a loan on a promissory note to pay the interest at the bank.

Varya.
If only God would help us!

Gayev.
On Tuesday I'll go and see about it again. (*To* VARYA.) Stop bawling. (*To* ANYA.) Your mamma will talk to Lopahin, and he, of course, will not refuse her . . . and as soon as you're rested, you'll go to Yaroslavl to the Countess, your great-aunt. So we'll be working in three directions at once, and the thing is in the bag. We'll pay the interest—I'm sure of it. (*Puts a candy in his mouth.*) I swear on my honor, I swear by anything you like, the estate shan't be sold. (*Excitedly.*) I swear by my own happiness! Here's my hand on it, you can call me a swindler and a scoundrel if I let it come to an auction! I swear by my whole being.

Anya.
(*Relieved and quite happy again.*) How good you are, Uncle, and how clever! (*Embraces him.*) Now I'm at peace, quite at peace, I'm happy.

(*Enter* FIRS.)

Firs.

(*Reproachfully.*) Leonid Andreyevich, have you no fear of God? When are you going to bed?

Gayev.

Directly, directly. Go away, Firs, I'll . . . yes, I will undress myself. Now, children, 'nightie-'nightie. We'll consider details tomorrow, but now go to sleep. (*Kisses* ANYA *and* VARYA.) I am a man of the eighties; they have nothing good to say of that period nowadays. Nevertheless, in the course of my life, I have suffered not a little for my convictions. It's not for nothing that the peasant loves me; one should know the peasant; one should know from which—

Anya.

There you go again, Uncle.

Varya.

Uncle dear, be quiet.

Firs.

(*Angrily.*) Leonid Andreyevich!

Gayev.

I'm coming, I'm coming! Go to bed! Double bank shot in the side pocket! Here goes a clean shot . . .

(*Exits,* FIRS *hobbling after him.*)

Anya.

I am at peace now. I don't want to go to Yaroslavl— I don't like my great-aunt, but still, I am at peace, thanks to Uncle. (*Sits down.*)

Varya.

We must get some sleep. I'm going now. While you were away, something unpleasant happened. In the old servants' quarters, there are only the old people as you know; Yefim, Polya, Yevstigney, and Karp, too. They began letting all sorts of rascals in to spend the night. . . . I didn't say anything. Then I heard they'd been spreading a report that I gave them nothing but dried peas to eat—out of stinginess, you know . . . and it was all Yevstigney's doing. . . . All right, I thought, if that's how it is, I thought, just wait. I sent for Yevstigney . . . (*Yawns.*) He comes. . . . "How's this, Yevstigney?" I say, "You fool . . ." (*Looking at* ANYA.) Anichka! (*Pauses.*) She's asleep. (*Puts her arm around* ANYA.) Come to your little bed. . . . Come . . . (*Leads her.*) My darling has fallen asleep. . . . Come.

(*They go out. Far away beyond the orchard, a shepherd is piping.* TROFIMOV *crosses the stage and, seeing* VARYA *and* ANYA, *stands still.*)

Varya.
Sh! She's asleep . . . asleep. . . . Come, darling.

Anya.
(*Softly, half-asleep.*) I'm so tired. Those bells . . . Uncle . . . dear. . . . Mamma and Uncle . . .

Varya.
Come, my precious, come along. (*They go into* ANYA'S *room.*)

Trofimov
(*With emotion.*) My sunshine, my spring!

ACT TWO

A meadow. An old, long-abandoned, lopsided little chapel; near it a well, large slabs, which had apparently once served as tombstones, and an old bench. In the background the road to the Gayev estate. To one side poplars loom darkly, where the cherry orchard begins. In the distance a row of telegraph poles, and far off, on the horizon, the faint outline of a large city which is seen only in fine, clear weather. The sun will soon be setting. CHARLOTTA, YASHA, *and* DUNYASHA *are seated on the bench.* YEPIHODOV *stands near and plays a guitar. All are pensive.* CHARLOTTA *wears an old peaked cap. She has taken a gun from her shoulder and is straightening the buckle on the strap.*

Charlotta.
(*Musingly.*) I haven't a real passport, I don't know how old I am, and I always feel that I am very young. When I was a little girl, my father and mother used to go from fair to fair and give performances, very good ones. And I used to do the *salto mortale,* and all sorts of other tricks. And when papa and mamma died, a German lady adopted me and began to educate me. Very good. I grew up and became a governess. But where I come from and who I am, I don't know. . . . Who were my parents? Perhaps they weren't even married. . . . I don't know . . . (*Takes a cucumber out*

49

of her pocket and eats it.) I don't know a thing.
(*Pause.*) One wants so much to talk, and there isn't
anyone to talk to. . . . I haven't anybody.

Yepihodov.

(*Plays the guitar and sings.*) "What care I for the
jarring world? What's friend or foe to me? . . ." How
agreeable it is to play the mandolin.

Dunyasha.

That's a guitar, not a mandolin. (*Looks in a hand
mirror and powders her face.*)

Yepihodov.

To a madman in love it's a mandolin. (*Sings.*) "Would
that the heart were warmed by the fire of mutual love!"
(YASHA *joins in.*)

Charlotta.

How abominably these people sing. Pfui! Like jackals!

Dunyasha.

(*To* YASHA.) How wonderful it must be though to have
stayed abroad!

Yasha.

Ah, yes, of course, I cannot but agree with you there.
(*Yawns and lights a cigar.*)

Yepihodov.

Naturally. Abroad, everything has long since achieved
full perplexion.

Yasha.

That goes without saying.

Yepihodov.

I'm a cultivated man, I read all kinds of remarkable
books. And yet I can never make out what direction I
should take, what is it that I want, properly speaking.
Should I live, or should I shoot myself, properly speaking? Nevertheless, I always carry a revolver about
me. . . . Here it is . . . (*Shows revolver.*)

Charlotta.

I've finished. I'm going. (*Puts the gun over her shoulder.*) You are a very clever man, Yepihodov, and a
very terrible one; women must be crazy about you.
Br-r-r! (*Starts to go.*) These clever men are all so
stupid; there's no one for me to talk to . . . always
alone, alone, I haven't a soul . . . and who I am, and

why I am, nobody knows. (*Exits unhurriedly.*)

Yepihodov.
Properly speaking and letting other subjects alone, I must say regarding myself, among other things, that fate treats me mercilessly, like a storm treats a small boat. If I am mistaken, let us say, why then do I wake up this morning, and there on my chest is a spider of enormous dimensions . . . like this . . . (*Indicates with both hands.*) Again, I take up a pitcher of kvass to have a drink, and in it there is something unseemly to the highest degree, something like a cockroach. (*Pause.*) Have you read Buckle? (*Pause.*) I wish to have a word with you, Avdotya Fyodorovna, if I may trouble you.

Dunyasha.
Well, go ahead.

Yepihodov.
I wish to speak with you alone. (*Sighs.*)

Dunyasha.
(*Embarrassed.*) Very well. Only first bring me my little cape. You'll find it near the wardrobe. It's rather damp here.

Yepihodov.
Certainly, ma'am; I will fetch it, ma'am. Now I know what to do with my revolver. (*Takes the guitar and goes off playing it.*)

Yasha.
Two-and-Twenty Troubles! An awful fool, between you and me. (*Yawns.*)

Dunyasha.
I hope to God he doesn't shoot himself! (*Pause.*) I've become so nervous, I'm always fretting. I was still a little girl when I was taken into the big house, I am quite unused to the simple life now, and my hands are white, as white as a lady's. I've become so soft, so delicate, so refined, I'm afraid of everything. It's so terrifying; and if you deceive me, Yasha, I don't know what will happen to my nerves. (YASHA *kisses her.*)

Yasha.
You're a peach! Of course, a girl should never forget herself; and what I dislike more than anything is when a girl don't behave properly.

Dunyasha.

I've fallen passionately in love with you; you're educated—you have something to say about everything.
(*Pause.*)

Yasha.

(*Yawns.*) Yes, ma'am. Now the way I look at it, if a
girl loves someone, it means she is immoral. (*Pause.*)
It's agreeable smoking a cigar in the fresh air.
(*Listens.*) Someone's coming this way. . . . It's our
madam and the others. (DUNYASHA *embraces him im-
pulsively.*) You go home, as though you'd been to the
river to bathe; go by the little path, or else they'll run
into you and suspect me of having arranged to meet
you here. I can't stand that sort of thing.

Dunyasha.

(*Coughing softly.*) Your cigar's made my head ache.
(*Exits.* YASHA *remains standing near the chapel. Enter*
MME. RANEVSKAYA, GAYEV, *and* LOPAHIN.)

Lopahin.

You must make up your mind once and for all—
there's no time to lose. It's quite a simple question,
you know. Do you agree to lease your land for summer cottages or not? Answer in one word, yes or no;
only one word!

Mme. Ranevskaya.

Who's been smoking such abominable cigars here?
(*Sits down.*)

Gayev.

Now that the railway line is so near, it's made things
very convenient. (*Sits down.*) Here we've been able
to have lunch in town. Yellow ball in the side pocket!
I feel like going into the house and playing just one
game.

Mme. Ranevskaya.

You can do that later.

Lopahin.

Only one word! (*Imploringly.*) Do give me an answer!

Gayev.

(*Yawning.*) Who?

Mme. Ranevskaya.

(*Looks into her purse.*) Yesterday I had a lot of
money and now my purse is almost empty. My poor

Varya tries to economize by feeding us just milk soup; in the kitchen the old people get nothing but dried peas to eat, while I squander money thoughtlessly. (*Drops the purse, scattering gold pieces.*) You see, there they go . . . (*Shows vexation.*)

Yasha.
Allow me—I'll pick them up. (*Picks up the money.*)

Mme. Ranevskaya.
Be so kind, Yasha. And why did I go to lunch in town? That nasty restaurant, with its music and the table-cloth smelling of soap. . . . Why drink so much, Leonid? Why eat so much? Why talk so much? Today again you talked a lot, and all so inappropriately about the seventies, about the decadents. And to whom? Talking to waiters about decadents!

Lopahin.
Yes.

Gayev.
(*Waving his hand.*) I'm incorrigible; that's obvious. (*Irritably, to* YASHA.) Why do you keep dancing about in front of me?

Yasha.
(*Laughs.*) I can't hear your voice without laughing—

Gayev.
Either he or I—

Mme. Ranevskaya.
Go away, Yasha; run along.

Yasha.
(*Handing* MME. RANEVSKAYA *her purse.*) I'm going, at once. (*Hardly able to suppress his laughter.*) This minute. (*Exits.*)

Lopahin.
That rich man, Deriganov, wants to buy your estate. They say he's coming to the auction himself.

Mme. Ranevskaya.
Where did you hear that?

Lopahin.
That's what they are saying in town.

Gayev.
Our aunt in Yaroslavl has promised to help; but when she will send the money, and how much, no one knows.

Lopahin.
How much will she send? A hundred thousand? Two hundred?

Mme. Ranevskaya.
Oh, well, ten or fifteen thousand; and we'll have to be grateful for that.

Lopahin.
Forgive me, but such frivolous people as you are, so queer and unbusinesslike—I never met in my life. One tells you in plain language that your estate is up for sale, and you don't seem to take it in.

Mme. Ranevskaya.
What are we to do? Tell us what to do.

Lopahin.
I do tell you, every day; every day I say the same thing! You must lease the cherry orchard and the land for summer cottages, you must do it and as soon as possible—right away. The auction is close at hand. Please understand! Once you've decided to have the cottages, you can raise as much money as you like, and you're saved.

Mme. Ranevskaya.
Cottages—summer people—forgive me, but it's all so vulgar.

Gayev.
I agree with you absolutely.

Lopahin.
I shall either burst into tears or scream or faint! I can't stand it! You've worn me out! (*To* GAYEV.) You're an old woman!

Gayev.
Who?

Lopahin.
An old woman! (*Gets up to go.*)

Mme. Ranevskaya.
(*Alarmed.*) No, don't go! Please stay, I beg you, my dear. Perhaps we shall think of something.

Lopahin.
What is there to think of?

Mme. Ranevskaya.
Don't go, I beg you. With you here it's more cheerful anyway. (*Pause.*) I keep expecting something to hap-

pen, it's as though the house were going to crash about our ears.

Gayev.

(*In deep thought.*) Bank shot in the corner. . . . Three cushions in the side pocket. . . .

Mme. Ranevskaya.

We have been great sinners . . .

Lopahin.

What sins could you have committed?

Gayev.

(*Putting a candy in his mouth.*) They say I've eaten up my fortune in candy! (*Laughs.*)

Mme. Ranevskaya.

Oh, my sins! I've squandered money away recklessly, like a lunatic, and I married a man who made nothing but debts. My husband drank himself to death on champagne, he was a terrific drinker. And then, to my sorrow, I fell in love with another man, and I lived with him. And just then—that was my first punishment —a blow on the head: my little boy was drowned here in the river. And I went abroad, went away forever . . . never to come back, never to see this river again . . . I closed my eyes and ran, out of my mind. . . . But he followed me, pitiless, brutal. I bought a villa near Mentone, because he fell ill there; and for three years, day and night, I knew no peace, no rest. The sick man wore me out, he sucked my soul dry. Then last year, when the villa was sold to pay my debts, I went to Paris, and there he robbed me, abandoned me, took up with another woman, I tried to poison myself —it was stupid, so shameful—and then suddenly I felt drawn back to Russia, back to my own country, to my little girl. (*Wipes her tears away.*) Lord, Lord! Be merciful, forgive me my sins—don't punish me any-more! (*Takes a telegram out of her pocket.*) This came today from Paris—he begs me to forgive him, implores me to go back . . . (*Tears up the telegram.*) Do I hear music? (*Listens.*)

Gayev.

That's our famous Jewish band, you remember? Four violins, a flute, and a double bass.

Mme. Ranevskaya.
Does it still exist? We ought to send for them some
evening and have a party.

Lopahin.
(*Listens.*) I don't hear anything. (*Hums softly.*) "The
Germans for a fee will Frenchify a Russian."
(*Laughs.*) I saw a play at the theater yesterday—
awfully funny.

Mme. Ranevskaya.
There was probably nothing funny about it. You
shouldn't go to see plays, you should look at yourselves
more often. How drab your lives are—how full of
unnecessary talk.

Lopahin.
That's true; come to think of it, we do live like fools.
(*Pause.*) My pop was a peasant, an idiot; he understood nothing, never taught me anything, all he did
was beat me when he was drunk, and always with
a stick. Fundamentally, I'm just the same kind of
blockhead and idiot. I was never taught anything—I
have a terrible handwriting, I write so that I feel
ashamed before people, like a pig.

Mme. Ranevskaya.
You should get married, my friend.

Lopahin.
Yes . . . that's true.

Mme. Ranevskaya.
To our Varya, she's a good girl.

Lopahin.
Yes.

Mme. Ranevskaya.
She's a girl who comes of simple people, she works
all day long; and above all, she loves you. Besides,
you've liked her for a long time now.

Lopahin.
Well, I've nothing against it. She's a good girl.
(*Pause.*)

Gayev.
I've been offered a place in the bank—6,000 a year.
Have you heard?

Mme. Ranevskaya.
You're not up to it. Stay where you are.

(FIRS *enters, carrying an overcoat.*)

Firs.
(*To* GAYEV.) Please put this on, sir, it's damp.

Gayev.
(*Putting it on.*) I'm fed up with you, brother.

Firs.
Never mind. This morning you drove off without saying a word. (*Looks him over.*)

Mme. Ranevskaya.
How you've aged, Firs.

Firs.
I beg your pardon?

Lopahin.
The lady says you've aged.

Firs.
I've lived a long time; they were arranging my wedding and your papa wasn't born yet. (*Laughs.*) When freedom came I was already head footman. I wouldn't consent to be set free then; I stayed on with the master . . . (*Pause.*) I remember they were all very happy, but why they were happy, they didn't know themselves.

Lopahin.
It was fine in the old days! At least there was flogging!

Firs.
(*Not hearing.*) Of course. The peasants kept to the masters, the masters kept to the peasants; but now they've all gone their own ways, and there's no making out anything.

Gayev.
Be quiet, Firs. I must go to town tomorrow. They've promised to introduce me to a general who might let us have a loan.

Lopahin.
Nothing will come of that. You won't even be able to pay the interest, you can be certain of that.

Mme. Ranevskaya.
He's raving, there isn't any general. (*Enter* TROFIMOV, ANYA, *and* VARYA.)

Gayev.
Here come our young people.

Anya.
There's Mamma, on the bench.

Mme. Ranevskaya.
(*Tenderly.*) Come here, come along, my darlings. (*Embraces* ANYA *and* VARYA.) If you only knew how I love you both! Sit beside me—there, like that. (*All sit down.*)

Lopahin.
Our perpetual student is always with the young ladies.

Trofimov.
That's not any of your business.

Lopahin.
He'll soon be fifty, and he's still a student!

Trofimov.
Stop your silly jokes.

Lopahin.
What are you so cross about, you queer bird?

Trofimov.
Oh, leave me alone.

Lopahin.
(*Laughs.*) Allow me to ask you, what do you think of me?

Trofimov.
What I think of you, Yermolay Alexeyevich, is this: you are a rich man who will soon be a millionaire. Well, just as a beast of prey, which devours everything that comes in its way, is necessary for the process of metabolism to go on, so you, too, are necessary. (*All laugh.*)

Varya.
Better tell us something about the planets, Petya.

Mme. Ranevskaya.
No, let's go on with yesterday's conversation.

Trofimov.
What was it about?

Gayev.
About man's pride.

Trofimov.
Yesterday we talked a long time, but we came to no conclusion. There is something mystical about man's pride in your sense of the word. Perhaps you're right, from your own point of view. But if you reason simply, without going into subtleties, then what call is there for pride? Is there any sense in it, if man is so poor a thing physiologically, and if, in the great majority

of cases, he is coarse, stupid, profoundly unhappy? We should stop admiring ourselves. We should work, and that's all.

Gayev.
You die, anyway.

Trofimov.
Who knows? And what does it mean—to die? Perhaps man has a hundred senses, and at his death only the five we know perish, while the other ninety-five remain alive.

Mme. Ranevskaya.
How clever you are, Petya!

Lopahin.
(*Ironically.*) Awfully clever!

Trofimov.
Mankind goes forward, developing its powers. Everything that is now unattainable for it will one day come within man's reach and be clear to him; only we must work, helping with all our might those who seek the truth. Here among us in Russia only the very few work as yet. The great majority of the intelligentsia, as far as I can see, seek nothing, do nothing, are totally unfit for work of any kind. They call themselves the intelligentsia, yet they are uncivil to their servants, treat the peasants like animals, are poor students, never read anything serious, do absolutely nothing at all, only talk about science, and have little appreciation of the arts. They are all solemn, have grim faces, they all philosophize and talk of weighty matters. And meanwhile the vast majority of us, ninety-nine out of a hundred, live like savages. At the least provocation—a punch in the jaw, and curses. They eat disgustingly, sleep in filth and stuffiness, bedbugs everywhere, stench and damp and moral slovenliness. And obviously, the only purpose of all our fine talk is to hoodwink ourselves and others. Show me where the public nurseries are that we've heard so much about, and the libraries. We read about them in novels, but in reality they don't exist, there is nothing but dirt, vulgarity, and Asiatic backwardness. I don't like very solemn

faces, I'm afraid of them, I'm afraid of serious conversations. We'd do better to keep quiet for a while.

Lopahin.
Do you know, I get up at five o'clock in the morning,
and I work from morning till night; and I'm always
handling money, my own and other people's, and I
see what people around me are really like. You've only
to start doing anything to see how few honest, decent
people there are. Sometimes when I lie awake at night,
I think: "Oh, Lord, thou hast given us immense for-
ests, boundless fields, the widest horizons, and living
in their midst, we ourselves ought really to be giants."

Mme. Ranevskaya.
Now you want giants! They're only good in fairy
tales; otherwise they're frightening.

(YEPIHODOV *crosses the stage at the rear, playing the
guitar.*)

Mme. Ranevskaya.
(*Pensively.*) There goes Yepihodov.

Anya.
(*Pensively.*) There goes Yepihodov.

Gayev.
Ladies and gentlemen, the sun has set.

Trofimov.
Yes.

Gayev.
(*In a low voice, declaiming as it were.*) Oh, Nature,
wondrous Nature, you shine with eternal radiance,
beautiful and indifferent! You, whom we call our
mother, unite within yourself life and death! You
animate and destroy!

Varya.
(*Pleadingly.*) Uncle dear!

Anya.
Uncle, again!

Trofimov.
You'd better bank the yellow ball in the side pocket.

Gayev.
I'm silent, I'm silent . . .

(*All sit plunged in thought. Stillness reigns. Only*

FIRS's *muttering is audible. Suddenly a distant sound is heard, coming from the sky as it were, the sound of a snapping string, mournfully dying away.*)

Mme. Ranevskaya.
What was that?

Lopahin.
I don't know. Somewhere far away, in the pits, a bucket's broken loose; but somewhere very far away.

Gayev.
Or it might be some sort of bird, perhaps a heron.

Trofimov.
Or an owl . . .

Mme. Ranevskaya.
(*Shudders.*) It's weird, somehow. (*Pause.*)

Firs.
Before the calamity the same thing happened—the owl screeched, and the samovar hummed all the time.

Gayev.
Before what calamity?

Firs.
Before the Freedom.[1] (*Pause.*)

Mme. Ranevskaya.
Come, my friends, let's be going. It's getting dark. (To ANYA.) You have tears in your eyes. What is it, my little one? (*Embraces her.*)

Anya.
I don't know, Mamma; it's nothing.

Trofimov.
Somebody's coming.

(*A* TRAMP *appears, wearing a shabby white cap and an overcoat. He is slightly drunk.*)

Tramp.
Allow me to inquire, will this shortcut take me to the station?

Gayev.
It will. Just follow that road.

Tramp.
My heartfelt thanks. (*Coughing.*) The weather is glorious. (*Recites.*) "My brother, my suffering brother.

[1] The emancipation of the serfs, proclaimed in 1861.

. . . Go down to the Volga! Whose groans . . . ?" (*To* VARYA.) Mademoiselle, won't you spare 30 kopecks for a hungry Russian?

Varya.
(*Frightened, cries out.*)

Lopahin.
(*Angrily.*) Even panhandling has its proprieties.

Mme. Ranevskaya.
(*Scared.*) Here, take this. (*Fumbles in her purse.*) I haven't any silver . . . never mind, here's a gold piece.

Tramp.
My heartfelt thanks. (*Exits. Laughter.*)

Varya.
(*Frightened.*) I'm leaving, I'm leaving. . . . Oh, Mamma dear, at home the servants have nothing to eat, and you gave him a gold piece!

Mme. Ranevskaya.
What are you going to do with me? I'm such a fool. When we get home, I'll give you everything I have. Yermolay Alexeyevich, you'll lend me some more . . .

Lopahin.
Yes, ma'am.

Mme. Ranevskaya.
Come, ladies and gentlemen, it's time to be going. Oh! Varya, we've settled all about your marriage. Congratulations!

Varya.
(*Through tears.*) Really, Mamma, that's not a joking matter.

Lopahin.
"Aurelia, get thee to a nunnery, go . . ."

Gayev.
And do you know, my hands are trembling: I haven't played billiards in a long time.

Lopahin.
"Aurelia, nymph, in your orisons, remember me!"

Mme. Ranevskaya.
Let's go, it's almost suppertime.

Varya.
He frightened me! My heart's pounding.

Lopahin.
Let me remind you, ladies and gentlemen, on the twenty-second of August the cherry orchard will be up for sale. Think about that! Think!

(*All except* TROFIMOV *and* ANYA *go out.*)

Anya.
(*Laughs.*) I'm grateful to that tramp, he frightened Varya and so we're alone.

Trofimov.
Varya's afraid we'll fall in love with each other all of a sudden. She hasn't left us alone for days. Her narrow mind can't grasp that we're above love. To avoid the petty and illusory, everything that prevents us from being free and happy—that is the goal and meaning of our life. Forward! Do not fall behind, friends!

Anya.
(*Strikes her hands together.*) How well you speak! (*Pause.*) It's wonderful here today.

Trofimov.
Yes, the weather's glorious.

Anya.
What have you done to me, Petya? Why don't I love the cherry orchard as I used to? I loved it so tenderly. It seemed to me there was no spot on earth lovelier than our orchard.

Trofimov.
All Russia is our orchard. Our land is vast and beautiful, there are many wonderful places in it. (*Pause.*) Think of it, Anya, your grandfather, your great-grandfather and all your ancestors were serf-owners, owners of living souls, and aren't human beings looking at you from every tree in the orchard, from every leaf, from every trunk? Don't you hear voices? Oh, it's terrifying! Your orchard is a fearful place, and when you pass through it in the evening or at night, the old bark on the trees gleams faintly, and the cherry trees seem to be dreaming of things that happened a hundred, two hundred years ago and to be tormented by painful visions. What is there to say? We're at least two hundred years behind, we've really achieved nothing yet, we have no definite attitude to the past, we only philosophize, complain of the blues, or drink vodka. It's all so clear: in order to live in the present,

we should first redeem our past, finish with it, and we can expiate it only by suffering, only by extraordinary, unceasing labor. Realize that, Anya.

Anya.
The house in which we live has long ceased to be our own, and I will leave it, I give you my word.

Trofimov.
If you have the keys, fling them into the well and go away. Be free as the wind.

Anya.
(*In ecstasy.*) How well you put that!

Trofimov.
Believe me, Anya, believe me! I'm not yet thirty, I'm young, I'm still a student—but I've already suffered so much. In winter I'm hungry, sick, harassed, poor as a beggar, and where hasn't Fate driven me? Where haven't I been? And yet always, every moment of the day and night, my soul is filled with inexplicable premonitions. . . . I have a premonition of happiness, Anya. . . . I see it already!

Anya.
(*Pensively.*) The moon is rising.

(YEPIHODOV *is heard playing the same mournful tune on the guitar. The moon rises. Somewhere near the poplars* VARYA *is looking for* ANYA *and calling,* "Anya, where are you?")

Trofimov.
Yes, the moon is rising. (*Pause.*) There it is, happiness, it's approaching, it's coming nearer and nearer, I can already hear its footsteps. And if we don't see it, if we don't know it, what does it matter? Others will!

Varya's voice.
Anya! Where are you?

Trofimov.
That Varya again! (*Angrily.*) It's revolting!

Anya.
Never mind, let's go down to the river. It's lovely there.

Trofimov.
Come on. (*They go.*)

Varya's voice.
Anya! Anya!

ACT THREE

A drawing room separated by an arch from a ballroom. Evening. Chandelier burning. The Jewish band is heard playing in the anteroom. In the ballroom they are dancing the Grand Rond. PISHCHIK *is heard calling,* "Promenade à une paire." PISHCHIK *and* CHARLOTTA, TROFIMOV *and* MME. RANEVSKAYA, ANYA *and the* POST OFFICE CLERK, VARYA *and the* STATION-MASTER, *and others enter the drawing room in couples.* DUNYASHA *is in the last couple.* VARYA *weeps quietly, wiping her tears as she dances. All parade through drawing room.* PISHCHIK *calling,* "Grand rond, balancez!" *and* "Les cavaliers à genoux et remerciez vos dames!" FIRS, *wearing a dress coat, brings in soda water on a tray.* PISHCHIK *and* TROFIMOV *enter the drawing room.*

Pishchik.
I'm a full-blooded man; I've already had two strokes. Dancing's hard work for me; but as they say, "If you run with the pack, you can bark or not, but at least wag your tail." Still, I'm as strong as a horse. My late lamented father, who would have his joke, God rest his soul, used to say, talking about our origin, that the ancient line of the Simeonov-Pishchiks was descended from the very horse that Caligula had made a senator. (*Sits down.*) But the trouble is, I have no

65

money. A hungry dog believes in nothing but meat. (*Snores, and wakes up at once.*) It's the same with me—I can think of nothing but money.

Trofimov.
You know, there *is* something equine about your figure.

Pishchik.
Well, a horse is a fine animal—one can sell a horse.

(*Sound of billiards being played in an adjoining room.* VARYA *appears in the archway.*)

Trofimov.
(*Teasing her.*) Madam Lopahina! Madam Lopahina!

Varya.
(*Angrily.*) Mangy master!

Trofimov.
Yes, I am a mangy master and I'm proud of it.

Varya.
(*Reflecting bitterly.*) Here we've hired musicians, and what shall we pay them with? (*Exits.*)

Trofimov.
(*To* PISHCHIK.) If the energy you have spent during your lifetime looking for money to pay interest had gone into something else, in the end you could have turned the world upside down.

Pishchik.
Nietzsche, the philosopher, the greatest, most famous of men, that colossal intellect, says in his works that it is permissible to forge banknotes.

Trofimov.
Have you read Nietzsche?

Pishchik.
Well . . . Dashenka told me. . . . And now I've got to the point where forging banknotes is about the only way out for me. . . . The day after tomorrow I have to pay 310 rubles—I already have 130 . . . (*Feels in his pockets. In alarm.*) The money's gone! I've lost my money! (*Through tears.*) Where's my money? (*Joyfully.*) Here it is! Inside the lining . . . I'm all in a sweat . . .

(*Enter* MME. RANEVSKAYA *and* CHARLOTTA.)

Mme. Ranevskaya.
(*Hums the "Lezginka."*) Why isn't Leonid back yet?
What is he doing in town? (*To* DUNYASHA.) Dunyasha,
offer the musicians tea.

Trofimov.
The auction hasn't taken place, most likely.

Mme. Ranevskaya.
It's the wrong time to have the band, and the wrong
time to give a dance. Well, never mind. (*Sits down
and hums softly.*)

Charlotta.
(*Hands* PISHCHIK *a pack of cards.*) Here is a pack of
cards. Think of any card you like.

Pishchik.
I've thought of one.

Charlotta.
Shuffle the pack now. That's right. Give it here, my
dear Mr. Pishchik. *Eins, zwei, drei!* Now look for it—
it's in your side pocket.

Pishchik.
(*Taking the card out of his pocket.*) The eight of
spades! Perfectly right! Just imagine!

Charlotta.
(*Holding pack of cards in her hands. To* TROFIMOV.)
Quickly, name the top card.

Trofimov.
Well, let's see—the queen of spades.

Charlotta.
Right! (*To* PISHCHIK.) Now name the top card.

Pishchik.
The ace of hearts.

Charlotta.
Right! (*Claps her hands and the pack of cards disappears.*) Ah, what lovely weather it is today! (*A
mysterious feminine voice, which seems to come from
under the floor, answers her:* "Oh, yes, it's magnificent
weather, madam.") You are my best ideal. (*Voice:*
"And I find you pleasing too, madam.")

Stationmaster.
(*Applauding.*) The lady ventriloquist, bravo!

Pishchik.

(*Amazed.*) Just imagine! Enchanting Charlotta Ivanovna, I'm simply in love with you.

Charlotta.

In love? (*Shrugs her shoulders.*) Are you capable of love? *Guter Mensch, aber schlechter Musikant!*

Trofimov.

(*Claps* PISHCHIK *on the shoulder.*) You old horse, you!

Charlotta.

Attention please! One more trick! (*Takes a plaid from a chair.*) Here is a very good plaid; I want to sell it. (*Shaking it out.*) Does anyone want to buy it?

Pishchik.

(*In amazement.*) Just imagine!

Charlotta.

Eins, zwei, drei! (*Raises the plaid quickly, behind it stands* ANYA. *She curtsies, runs to her mother, embraces her, and runs back into the ballroom, amid general enthusiasm.*)

Mme. Ranevskaya.

(*Applauds.*) Bravo! Bravo!

Charlotta.

Now again! *Eins, zwei, drei!* (*Lifts the plaid; behind it stands* VARYA, *bowing.*)

Pishchik.

(*In amazement.*) Just imagine!

Charlotta.

The end! (*Throws the plaid at* PISHCHIK, *curtsies, and runs into the ballroom.*)

Pishchik.

(*Running after her.*) The rascal! What a woman, what a woman! (*Exits.*)

Mme. Ranevskaya.

And Leonid still isn't here. What is he doing in town so long? I don't understand. It must be all over by now. Either the estate has been sold, or the auction hasn't taken place. Why keep us in suspense so long?

Varya.

(*Trying to console her.*) Uncle's bought it, I feel sure of that.

Trofimov.

(*Mockingly.*) Oh, yes!

Varya.
Great-aunt sent him an authorization to buy it in her name, and to transfer the debt. She's doing it for Anya's sake. And I'm sure that God will help us, and Uncle will buy it.

Mme. Ranevskaya.
Great-aunt sent fifteen thousand to buy the estate in her name, she doesn't trust us, but that's not even enough to pay the interest. (*Covers her face with her hands.*) Today my fate will be decided, my fate—

Trofimov.
(*Teasing* VARYA.) Madam Lopahina!

Varya.
(*Angrily.*) Perpetual student! Twice already you've been expelled from the university.

Mme. Ranevskaya.
Why are you so cross, Varya? He's teasing you about Lopahin. Well, what of it? If you want to marry Lopahin, go ahead. He's a good man, and interesting; if you don't want to, don't. Nobody's compelling you, my pet!

Varya.
Frankly, Mamma dear, I take this thing seriously; he's a good man and I like him.

Mme. Ranevskaya.
All right then, marry him. I don't know what you're waiting for.

Varya.
But, Mamma, I can't propose to him myself. For the last two years, everyone's been talking to me about him—talking. But he either keeps silent, or else cracks jokes. I understand; he's growing rich, he's absorbed in business—he has no time for me. If I had money, even a little, say, 100 rubles, I'd throw everything up and go far away—I'd go into a nunnery.

Trofimov.
What a blessing ...

Varya.
A student ought to be intelligent. (*Softly, with tears in her voice.*) How homely you've grown, Petya! How old you look! (*To* MME. RANEVSKAYA, *with dry eyes.*)

But I can't live without work, Mamma dear; I must keep busy every minute.

(*Enter* YASHA.)

Yasha.

(*Hardly restraining his laughter.*) Yepihodov has broken a billiard cue! (*Exits.*)

Varya.

Why is Yepihodov here? Who allowed him to play billiards? I don't understand these people! (*Exits.*)

Mme. Ranevskaya.

Don't tease her, Petya. She's unhappy enough without that.

Trofimov.

She bustles so—and meddles in other people's business. All summer long she's given Anya and me no peace. She's afraid of a love affair between us. What business is it of hers? Besides, I've given no grounds for it, and I'm far from such vulgarity. We are above love.

Mme. Ranevskaya.

And I suppose I'm beneath love? (*Anxiously.*) What can be keeping Leonid? If I only knew whether the estate has been sold or not. Such a calamity seems so incredible to me that I don't know what to think—I feel lost. . . . I could scream. . . . I could do something stupid. . . . Save me, Petya, tell me something, talk to me!

Trofimov.

Whether the estate is sold today or not, isn't it all one? That's all done with long ago—there's no turning back, the path is overgrown. Calm yourself, my dear. You mustn't deceive yourself. For once in your life you must face the truth.

Mme. Ranevskaya.

What truth? You can see the truth, you can tell it from falsehood, but I seem to have lost my eyesight, I see nothing. You settle every great problem so boldly, but tell me, my dear boy, isn't it because you're young, because you don't yet know what one of your problems means in terms of suffering? You look ahead fearlessly, but isn't it because you don't see and don't expect anything dreadful, because life is still hidden from your young eyes? You're bolder, more honest, more profound than we are, but think hard, show just a bit of magnanimity, spare me. After all, I was born here, my father and mother lived here, and my grandfather; I love this house. Without the cherry orchard, my life has no meaning for me, and if it really must be sold, then sell me with the orchard. (*Embraces* TROFIMOV, *kisses him on the forehead.*) My son was drowned here. (*Weeps.*) Pity me, you good, kind fellow!

Trofimov.
You know, I feel for you with all my heart.

Mme. Ranevskaya.
But that should have been said differently, so differently! (*Takes out her handkerchief—a telegram falls on the floor.*) My heart is so heavy today—you can't imagine! The noise here upsets me—my inmost being trembles at every sound—I'm shaking all over. But I can't go into my own room; I'm afraid to be alone. Don't condemn me, Petya. . . . I love you as though you were one of us, I would gladly let you marry Anya—I swear I would—only, my dear boy, you must study—you must take your degree—you do nothing, you let yourself be tossed by Fate from place to place—it's so strange. It's true, isn't it? And you should do something about your beard, to make it grow somehow! (*Laughs.*) You're so funny!

Trofimov.
(*Picks up the telegram.*) I've no wish to be a dandy.

Mme. Ranevskaya.
That's a telegram from Paris. I get one every day. One yesterday and one today. That savage is ill again —he's in trouble again. He begs forgiveness, implores me to go to him, and really I ought to go to Paris to be near him. Your face is stern, Petya; but what is there to do, my dear boy? What am I to do? He's ill, he's alone and unhappy, and who is to look after him, who is to keep him from doing the wrong thing, who is to give him his medicine on time? And why hide

it or keep still about it—I love him! That's clear. I love him, love him! He's a millstone round my neck, he'll drag me to the bottom, but I love that stone, I can't live without it. (*Presses* TROFIMOV's *hand*.) Don't think badly of me, Petya, and don't say anything, don't say . . .

Trofimov.
(*Through tears*.) Forgive me my frankness in heaven's name; but, you know, he robbed you!

Mme. Ranevskaya.
No, no, no, you mustn't say such things! (*Covers her ears*.)

Trofimov.
But he's a scoundrel! You're the only one who doesn't know it. He's a petty scoundrel—a nonentity!

Mme. Ranevskaya.
(*Controlling her anger*.) You are twenty-six or twenty-seven years old, but you're still a schoolboy.

Trofimov.
That may be.

Mme. Ranevskaya.
You should be a man at your age. You should understand people who love—and ought to be in love yourself. You ought to fall in love! (*Angrily*.) Yes, yes! And it's not purity in you, it's prudishness, you're simply a queer fish, a comical freak!

Trofimov.
(*Horrified*.) What is she saying?

Mme. Ranevskaya.
"I am above love!" You're not above love, but simply, as our Firs says, you're an addlehead. At your age not to have a mistress!

Trofimov.
(*Horrified*.) This is frightful! What is she saying! (*Goes rapidly into the ballroom, clutching his head*.) It's frightful—I can't stand it, I won't stay! (*Exits, but returns at once*.) All is over between us! (*Exits into anteroom*.)

Mme. Ranevskaya.
(*Shouts after him*.) Petya! Wait! You absurd fellow, I was joking. Petya!

(*Sound of somebody running quickly downstairs*

and suddenly falling down with a crash. ANYA *and* VARYA *scream. Sound of laughter a moment later.*)

Mme. Ranevskaya.
What's happened?

(ANYA *runs in.*)

Anya.
(*Laughing.*) Petya's fallen downstairs! (*Runs out.*)
Mme. Ranevskaya.
What a queer bird that Petya is!

(STATIONMASTER, *standing in the middle of the ballroom, recites Alexey Tolstoy's "Magdalene," to which all listen, but after a few lines, the sound of a waltz is heard from the anteroom and the reading breaks off. All dance.* TROFIMOV, ANYA, VARYA, *and* MME. RANEVSKAYA *enter from the anteroom.*)

Mme. Ranevskaya.
Petya, you pure soul, please forgive me. . . . Let's dance.

(*Dances with* PETYA. ANYA *and* VARYA *dance.* FIRS *enters, puts his stick down by the side door.* YASHA *enters from the drawing room and watches the dancers.*)

Yasha.
Well, Grandfather?
Firs.
I'm not feeling well. In the old days it was generals, barons, and admirals that were dancing at our balls, and now we have to send for the Post Office Clerk and the Stationmaster, and even they aren't too glad to come. I feel kind of shaky. The old master that's gone, their grandfather, dosed everyone with sealing wax, whatever ailed 'em. I've been taking sealing wax every day for twenty years or more. Perhaps that's what's kept me alive.
Yasha.
I'm fed up with you, Grandpop. (*Yawns.*) It's time you croaked.
Firs.
Oh, you addlehead! (*Mumbles.*)

(TROFIMOV *and* MME. RANEVSKAYA *dance from the ballroom into the drawing room.*)

Mme. Ranevskaya.
Merci. I'll sit down a while. (*Sits down.*) I'm tired.

(*Enter* ANYA.)

Anya.
(*Excitedly.*) There was a man in the kitchen just now who said the cherry orchard was sold today.

Mme. Ranevskaya.
Sold to whom?

Anya.
He didn't say. He's gone. (*Dances off with* TROFI-MOV.)

Yasha.
It was some old man gabbing, a stranger.

Firs.
And Leonid Andreyevich isn't back yet, he hasn't come. And he's wearing his lightweight between-season overcoat; like enough, he'll catch cold. Ah, when they're young they're green.

Mme. Ranevskaya.
This is killing me. Go, Yasha, find out to whom it has been sold.

Yasha.
But the old man left long ago. (*Laughs.*)

Mme. Ranevskaya.
What are you laughing at? What are you pleased about?

Yasha.
That Yepihodov is such a funny one. A funny fellow, Two-and-Twenty Troubles!

Mme. Ranevskaya.
Firs, if the estate is sold, where will you go?

Firs.
I'll go where you tell me.

Mme. Ranevskaya.
Why do you look like that? Are you ill? You ought to go to bed.

Firs.
Yes! (*With a snigger.*) Me go to bed, and who's to hand things round? Who's to see to things? I'm the only one in the whole house.

Yasha.
(*To* MME. RANEVSKAYA.) Lubov Andreyevna, allow
me to ask a favor of you, be so kind! If you go back to
Paris, take me with you, I beg you. It's positively
impossible for me to stay here. (*Looking around;
sotto voce.*) What's the use of talking? You see for
yourself, it's an uncivilized country, the people have
no morals, and then the boredom! The food in the
kitchen's revolting, and besides there's this Firs wan-
ders about mumbling all sorts of inappropriate words.
Take me with you, be so kind!

(*Enter* PISHCHIK.)

Pishchik.
May I have the pleasure of a waltz with you, charming lady? (MME. RANEVSKAYA *accepts.*) All the same,
enchanting lady, you must let me have 180 rubles. . . .
You must let me have (*dancing*) just one hundred
and eighty rubles. (*They pass into the ballroom.*)

Yasha.
(*Hums softly.*) "Oh, wilt thou understand the tumult
in my soul?"

(*In the ballroom a figure in a gray top hat and
checked trousers is jumping about and waving its
arms; shouts:* "Bravo, Charlotta Ivanovna!")

Dunyasha.
(*Stopping to powder her face; to* FIRS.) The young
miss has ordered me to dance. There are so many
gentlemen and not enough ladies. But dancing makes
me dizzy, my heart begins to beat fast, Firs Nikolaye-
vich. The Post Office Clerk said something to me just
now that quite took my breath away. (*Music stops.*)

Firs.
What did he say?

Dunyasha.
"You're like a flower," he said.

Yasha.
(*Yawns.*) What ignorance. (*Exits.*)

Dunyasha.
"Like a flower!" I'm such a delicate girl. I simply
adore pretty speeches.

Firs.
You'll come to a bad end.
(*Enter* YEPIHODOV.)

Yepihodov.
(*To* DUNYASHA.) You have no wish to see me, Avdotya
Fyodorovna . . . as though I was some sort of insect.
(*Sighs.*) Ah, life!

Dunyasha.
What is it you want?

Yepihodov.
Indubitably you may be right. (*Sighs.*) But of course,
if one looks at it from the point of view, if I may be
allowed to say so, and apologizing for my frankness,
you have completely reduced me to a state of mind.
I know my fate. Every day some calamity befalls me,
and I grew used to it long ago, so that I look upon my
fate with a smile. You gave me your word, and
though I—

Dunyasha.
Let's talk about it later, please. But just now leave
me alone, I am daydreaming. (*Plays with a fan.*)

Yepihodov.
A misfortune befalls me every day; and if I may be
allowed to say so, I merely smile, I even laugh.

(*Enter* VARYA.)

Varya.
(*To* YEPIHODOV.) Are you still here? What an im-
pertinent fellow you are really! Run along, Dunyasha.
(*To* YEPIHODOV.) Either you're playing billiards and
breaking a cue, or you're wandering about the drawing room as though you were a guest.

Yepihodov.
You cannot, permit me to remark, penalize me.

Varya.
I'm not penalizing you; I'm just telling you. You
merely wander from place to place, and don't do
your work. We keep you as a clerk, but heaven knows
what for.

Yepihodov.
(*Offended.*) Whether I work or whether I walk,

whether I eat or whether I play billiards, is a matter to be discussed only by persons of understanding and of mature years.

Varya.
(*Enraged.*) You dare say that to me—you dare? You mean to say I've no understanding? Get out of here at once! This minute!

Yepihodov.
(*Scared.*) I beg you to express yourself delicately.

Varya.
(*Beside herself.*) Clear out this minute! Out with you!

(YEPIHODOV *goes toward the door,* VARYA *following.*)

Varya.
Two-and-Twenty Troubles! Get out—don't let me set eyes on you again!

(*Exit* YEPIHODOV. *His voice is heard behind the door:* "I shall lodge a complaint against you!")

Varya.
Oh, you're coming back? (*She seizes the stick left near door by* FIRS.) Well, come then . . . come . . . I'll show you. . . . Ah, you're coming? You're coming? . . . Come . . . (*Swings the stick just as* LOPAHIN *enters.*)

Lopahin.
Thank you kindly.

Varya.
(*Angrily and mockingly.*) I'm sorry.

Lopahin.
It's nothing. Thank you kindly for your charming reception.

Varya.
Don't mention it. (*Walks away, looks back and asks softly.*) I didn't hurt you, did I?

Lopahin.
Oh, no, not at all. I shall have a large bump, though.

(*Voices from the ballroom:* "Lopahin is here! Lopahin!")

(*Enter* PISHCHIK.)

Pishchik.
My eyes do see, my ears do hear! (*Kisses* LOPAHIN.)

Lopahin.
You smell of cognac, my dear friends. And we've been celebrating here, too.

(*Enter* MME. RANEVSKAYA.)

Mme. Ranevskaya.
Is that you, Yermolay Alexeyevich? What kept you so long? Where's Leonid?

Lopahin.
Leonid Andreyevich arrived with me. He's coming.

Mme. Ranevskaya.
Well, what happened? Did the sale take place? Speak!

Lopahin.
(*Embarrassed, fearful of revealing his joy.*) The sale was over at four o'clock. We missed the train—had to wait till half-past nine. (*Sighing heavily.*) Ugh. I'm a little dizzy.

(*Enter* GAYEV. *In his right hand he holds parcels, with his left he is wiping away his tears.*)

Mme. Ranevskaya.
Well, Leonid? What news? (*Impatiently, through tears.*) Be quick, for God's sake!

Gayev.
(*Not answering, simply waves his hand. Weeping, to* FIRS.) Here, take these; anchovies, Kerch herrings ... I haven't eaten all day. What I've been through! (*The click of billiard balls comes through the open door of the billiard room and* YASHA'*s voice is heard:* "Seven and eighteen!" GAYEV'*s expression changes, he no longer weeps.*) I'm terribly tired. Firs, help me change. (*Exits, followed by* FIRS.)

Pishchik.
How about the sale? Tell us what happened.

Mme. Ranevskaya.
Is the cherry orchard sold?

Lopahin.
Sold.

Mme. Ranevskaya.
Who bought it?

Lopahin.
I bought it.

(*Pause.* MME. RANEVSKAYA *is overcome. She would fall to the floor, were it not for the chair and table near which she stands.* VARYA *takes the keys from her belt, flings them on the floor in the middle of the drawing room and goes out.*)

Lopahin.
I bought it. Wait a bit, ladies and gentlemen, please, my head is swimming, I can't talk. (*Laughs.*) We got to the auction and Deriganov was there already. Leonid Andreyevich had only 15,000 and straight off Deriganov bid 30,000 over and above the mortgage. I saw how the land lay, got into the fight, bid 40,000. He bid 45,000. I bid fifty-five. He kept adding five thousands, I ten. Well . . . it came to an end. I bid ninety above the mortgage and the estate was knocked down to me. Now the cherry orchard's mine! Mine! (*Laughs uproariously.*) Lord! God in Heaven! The cherry orchard's mine! Tell me that I'm drunk—out of my mind—that it's all a dream. (*Stamps his feet.*) Don't laugh at me! If my father and my grandfather could rise from their graves and see all that has happened—how their Yermolay, who used to be flogged, their half-literate Yermolay, who used to run about barefoot in winter, how that very Yermolay has bought the most magnificent estate in the world. I bought the estate where my father and grandfather were slaves, where they weren't even allowed to enter the kitchen. I'm asleep—it's only a dream—I only imagine it. . . . It's the fruit of your imagination, wrapped in the darkness of the unknown! (*Picks up the keys, smiling genially.*) She threw down the keys, wants to show she's no longer mistress here. (*Jingles keys.*) Well, no matter. (*The band is heard tuning up.*) Hey, musicians! Strike up! I want to hear you! Come, everybody, and see how Yermolay Lopahin will lay the ax to the cherry orchard and how the trees will fall to the ground. We will build summer cottages there, and our grandsons and great-grandsons will see a new life here. Music! Strike up!

(*The band starts to play.* MME. RANEVSKAYA *has sunk into a chair and is weeping bitterly.*)

Lopahin.

(*Reproachfully.*) Why, why didn't you listen to me? My dear friend, my poor friend, you can't bring it back now. (*Tearfully.*) Oh, if only this were over quickly! Oh, if only our wretched, disordered life were changed!

Pishchik.

(*Takes him by the arm; sotto voce.*) She's crying. Let's go into the ballroom. Let her be alone. Come. (*Takes his arm and leads him into the ballroom.*)

Lopahin.

What's the matter? Musicians, play so I can hear you! Let me have things the way I want them. (*Ironically.*) Here comes the new master, the owner of the cherry orchard. (*Accidentally he trips over a little table, almost upsetting the candelabra.*) I can pay for everything. (*Exits with* PISHCHIK.)

(MME. RANEVSKAYA, *alone, sits huddled up, weeping bitterly. Music plays softly. Enter* ANYA *and* TROFIMOV *quickly.* ANYA *goes to her mother and falls on her knees before her.* TROFIMOV *stands in the doorway.*)

Anya.

Mamma, Mamma, you're crying! Dear, kind, good Mamma, my precious, I love you, I bless you! The cherry orchard is sold, it's gone, that's true, quite true. But don't cry, Mamma, life is still before you, you still have your kind, pure heart. Let us go, let us go away from here, darling. We will plant a new orchard, even more luxuriant than this one. You will see it, you will understand, and like the sun at evening, joy—deep, tranquil joy—will sink into your soul, and you will smile, Mamma. Come, darling, let us go.

ACT FOUR

Scene as in Act One. No window curtains or pictures, only a little furniture, piled up in a corner, as if for sale. A sense of emptiness. Near the outer door and at the back, suitcases, bundles, etc., are piled up. A door open on the left and the voices of VARYA *and* ANYA *are heard.* LOPAHIN *stands waiting.* YASHA *holds a tray with glasses full of champagne.* YEPIHODOV *in the anteroom is tying up a box. Behind the scene a hum of voices: peasants have come to say good-bye. Voice of* GAYEV: "Thanks, brothers, thank you."

Yasha.
The country folk have come to say good-bye. In my opinion, Yermolay Alexeyevich, they are kindly souls, but there's nothing in their heads.

> (*The hum dies away. Enter* MME. RANEVSKAYA *and* GAYEV. *She is not crying, but is pale, her face twitches and she cannot speak.*)

Gayev.
You gave them your purse, Luba. That won't do! That won't do!

Mme. Ranevskaya.
I couldn't help it! I couldn't! (*They go out.*)

Lopahin.
(*Calls after them.*) Please, I beg you, have a glass at parting. I didn't think of bringing any champagne

from town and at the station I could find only one
bottle. Please, won't you? (*Pause.*) What's the matter,
ladies and gentlemen, don't you want any? (*Moves
away from the door.*) If I'd known, I wouldn't have
bought it. Well, then I won't drink any, either. (YASHA
carefully sets the tray down on a chair.) At least you
have a glass, Yasha.

Yasha.
Here's to the travelers! And good luck to those that
stay! (*Drinks.*) This champagne isn't the real stuff,
I can assure you.

Lopahin.
Eight rubles a bottle. (*Pause.*) It's devilishly cold here.

Yasha.
They didn't light the stoves today—it wasn't worth it,
since we're leaving. (*Laughs.*)

Lopahin.
Why are you laughing?

Yasha.
It's just that I'm pleased.

Lopahin.
It's October, yet it's as still and sunny as though it
were summer. Good weather for building. (*Looks at
his watch, and speaks off.*) Bear in mind, ladies and
gentlemen, the train goes in forty-seven minutes, so
you ought to start for the station in twenty minutes.
Better hurry up!

(*Enter* TROFIMOV, *wearing an overcoat.*)

Trofimov.
I think it's time to start. The carriages are at the door.
The devil only knows what's become of my rubbers;
they've disappeared. (*Calling off.*) Anya! My rubbers
are gone. I can't find them.

Lopahin.
I've got to go to Kharkov. I'll take the same train you
do. I'll spend the winter in Kharkov. I've been hang-
ing round here with you, till I'm worn out with loafing.
I can't live without work—I don't know what to do
with my hands, they dangle as if they didn't belong
to me.

Trofimov.
Well, we'll soon be gone, then you can go on with your useful labors again.

Lopahin.
Have a glass.

Trofimov.
No, I won't.

Lopahin.
So you're going to Moscow now?

Trofimov.
Yes. I'll see them into town, and tomorrow I'll go on to Moscow.

Lopahin.
Well, I'll wager the professors aren't giving any lectures, they're waiting for you to come.

Trofimov.
That's none of your business.

Lopahin.
Just how many years have you been at the university?

Trofimov.
Can't you think of something new? Your joke's stale and flat. (*Looking for his rubbers.*) We'll probably never see each other again, so allow me to give you a piece of advice at parting: don't wave your hands about! Get out of the habit. And another thing: building bungalows, figuring that summer residents will eventually become small farmers, figuring like that is just another form of waving your hands about.... Never mind, I love you anyway; you have fine, delicate fingers, like an artist; you have a fine, delicate soul.

Lopahin.
(*Embracing him.*) Good-bye, my dear fellow. Thank you for everything. Let me give you some money for the journey, if you need it.

Trofimov.
What for? I don't need it.

Lopahin.
But you haven't any.

Trofimov.
Yes, I have, thank you. I got some money for a translation—here it is in my pocket. (*Anxiously.*) But where are my rubbers?

Varya.

(*From the next room.*) Here! Take the nasty things. (*Flings a pair of rubbers onto the stage.*)

Trofimov.

What are you so cross about, Varya? Hm ... and these are not my rubbers.

Lopahin.

I sowed three thousand acres of poppies in the spring, and now I've made 40,000 on them, clear profit; and when my poppies were in bloom, what a picture it was! So, as I say, I made 40,000; and I am offering you a loan because I can afford it. Why turn up your nose at it? I'm a peasant—I speak bluntly.

Trofimov.

Your father was a peasant, mine was a druggist—that proves absolutely nothing whatever (LOPAHIN *takes out his wallet.*) Don't, put that away! If you were to offer me two hundred thousand, I wouldn't take it. I'm a free man. And everything that all of you, rich and poor alike, value so highly and hold so dear hasn't the slightest power over me. It's like so much fluff floating in the air. I can get on without you, I can pass you by, I'm strong and proud. Mankind is moving toward the highest truth, toward the highest happiness possible on earth, and I am in the front ranks.

Lopahin.

Will you get there?

Trofimov.

I will. (*Pause.*) I will get there, or I will show others the way to get there.

(*The sound of axes chopping down trees is heard in the distance.*)

Lopahin.

Well, good-bye, my dear fellow. It's time to leave. We turn up our noses at one another, but life goes on just the same. When I'm working hard, without resting, my mind is easier, and it seems to me that I, too, know why I exist. But how many people are there in Russia, brother, who exist nobody knows why? Well, it doesn't matter. That's not what makes the wheels go round. They say Leonid Andreyevich has taken a position in the bank, 6,000 rubles a year. Only, of course, he won't stick to it, he's too lazy. . . .

Anya.
(*In the doorway.*) Mamma begs you not to start cutting down the cherry trees until she's gone.

Trofimov.
Really, you should have more tact! (*Exits.*)

Lopahin.
Right away—right away! Those men . . . (*Exits.*)

Anya.
Has Firs been taken to the hospital?

Yasha.
I told them this morning. They must have taken him.

Anya.
(*To* YEPIHODOV, *who crosses the room.*) Yepihodov, please find out if Firs has been taken to the hospital.

Yasha.
(*Offended.*) I told Yegor this morning. Why ask a dozen times?

Yepihodov.
The aged Firs, in my definitive opinion, is beyond mending. It's time he was gathered to his fathers. And I can only envy him. (*Puts a suitcase down on a hat-box and crushes it.*) There now, of course. I knew it! (*Exits.*)

Yasha.
(*Mockingly.*) Two-and-Twenty Troubles!

Varya.
(*Through the door.*) Has Firs been taken to the hospital?

Anya.
Yes.

Varya.
Then why wasn't the note for the doctor taken too?

Anya.
Oh! Then someone must take it to him. (*Exits.*)

Varya.
(*From adjoining room.*) Where's Yasha? Tell him his mother's come and wants to say good-bye.

Yasha.
(*Waves his hand.*) She tries my patience.

(DUNYASHA *has been occupied with the luggage. Seeing* YASHA *alone, she goes up to him.*)

Dunyasha.

You might just give me one little look, Yasha. You're going away.... You're leaving me ... (*Weeps and throws herself on his neck.*)

Yasha.

What's there to cry about? (*Drinks champagne.*) In six days I shall be in Paris again. Tomorrow we get into an express train and off we go, that's the last you'll see of us.... I can scarcely believe it. *Vive la France!* It don't suit me here, I just can't live here. That's all there is to it. I'm fed up with the ignorance here, I've had enough of it. (*Drinks champagne.*) What's there to cry about? Behave yourself properly, and you'll have no cause to cry.

Dunyasha.

(*Powders her face, looking in pocket mirror.*) Do send me a letter from Paris. You know I loved you, Yasha, how I loved you! I'm a delicate creature, Yasha.

Yasha.

Somebody's coming! (*Busies himself with the luggage; hums softly.*)

(*Enter* MME. RANEVSKAYA, GAYEV, ANYA, *and* CHAR-LOTTA.)

Gayev.

We ought to be leaving. We haven't much time. (*Looks at* YASHA.) Who smells of herring?

Mme. Ranevskaya.

In about ten minutes we should be getting into the carriages. (*Looks around the room.*) Good-bye, dear old home, good-bye, grandfather. Winter will pass, spring will come, you will no longer be here, they will have torn you down. How much these walls have seen! (*Kisses* ANYA *warmly.*) My treasure, how radiant you look! Your eyes are sparkling like diamonds. Are you glad? Very?

Anya.

(*Gaily.*) Very glad. A new life is beginning, Mamma.

Gayev.
Well, really, everything is all right now. Before the cherry orchard was sold, we all fretted and suffered; but afterward, when the question was settled finally and irrevocably, we all calmed down, and even felt quite cheerful. I'm a bank employee now, a financier. The yellow ball in the side pocket! And anyhow, you are looking better Luba, there's no doubt of that.

Mme. Ranevskaya.
Yes, my nerves are better, that's true. (*She is handed her hat and coat.*) I sleep well. Carry out my things, Yasha. It's time. (*To* ANYA.) We shall soon see each other again, my little girl. I'm going to Paris, I'll live there on the money your great-aunt sent us to buy the estate with—long live Auntie! But that money won't last long.

Anya.
You'll come back soon, soon, Mamma, won't you? Meanwhile I'll study, I'll pass my high school examination, and then I'll go to work and help you. We'll read all kinds of books together, Mamma, won't we? (*Kisses her mother's hands.*) We'll read in the autumn evenings, we'll read lots of books, and a new wonderful world will open up before us. (*Falls into a revery.*) Mamma, do come back.

Mme. Ranevskaya.
I will come back, my precious. (*Embraces her daughter. Enter* LOPAHIN *and* CHARLOTTA *who is humming softly.*)

Gayev.
Charlotta's happy: she's singing.

Charlotta.
(*Picks up a bundle and holds it like a baby in swaddling clothes.*) Bye, baby, bye. (*A baby is heard crying:* "Wah! Wah!") Hush, hush, my pet, my little one. ("Wah! Wah!") I'm so sorry for you! (*Throws the bundle down.*) You will find me a position, won't you? I can't go on like this.

Lopahin.
We'll find one for you, Charlotta Ivanovna, don't worry.

Gayev.
Everyone's leaving us. Varya's going away. We've suddenly become of no use.

Charlotta.
There's no place for me to live in town, I must go away. (*Hums.*)

(*Enter* PISHCHIK.)

Lopahin.
There's nature's masterpiece!

Pishchik.
(*Gasping.*) Oh . . . let me get my breath . . . I'm in agony. . . . Esteemed friends . . . Give me a drink of water. . . .

Gayev.
Wants some money, I suppose. No, thank you . . . I'll keep out of harm's way. (*Exits.*)

Pishchik.
It's a long while since I've been to see you, most charming lady. (*To* LOPAHIN.) So you are here . . . glad to see you, you intellectual giant . . . There . . . (*Gives* LOPAHIN *money.*) Here's 400 rubles, and I still owe you 840.

Lopahin.
(*Shrugging his shoulders in bewilderment.*) I must be dreaming. . . . Where did you get it?

Pishchik.
Wait a minute . . . it's hot. . . . A most extraordinary event! Some Englishmen came to my place and found some sort of white clay on my land . . . (*To* MME. RANEVSKAYA.) And 400 for you . . . most lovely . . . most wonderful . . . (*Hands her the money.*) The rest later. (*Drinks water.*) A young man in the train was telling me just now that a great philosopher recommends jumping off roofs. "Jump!" says he; "that's the long and the short of it!" (*In amazement.*) Just imagine! Some more water!

Lopahin.
What Englishmen?

Pishchik.
I leased them the tract with the clay on it for twenty-four years. . . . And now, forgive me, I can't stay. . . .

I must be dashing on. . . . I'm going over to Znoikov
. . . to Kardamanov . . . I owe them all money . . .
(*Drinks water.*) Good-bye, everybody . . . I'll look in
on Thursday . . .

Mme. Ranevskaya.
We're just moving into town; and tomorrow I go
abroad.

Pishchik.
(*Upset.*) What? Why into town? That's why the furniture is like that . . . and the suitcases. . . . Well, never
mind! (*Through tears.*) Never mind . . . men of
colossal intellect, these Englishmen. . . . Never mind
. . . Be happy. God will come to your help. . . . Never
mind . . . everything in this world comes to an end.
(*Kisses* MME. RANEVSKAYA'S *hand.*) If the rumor
reaches you that it's all up with me, remember this
old . . . horse, and say: "Once there lived a certain
. . . Simeonov-Pishchik . . . the kingdom of Heaven
be his. . . ." Glorious weather! . . . Yes . . . (*Exits, in
great confusion, but at once returns and says in the
doorway.*) My daughter Dashenka sends her regards.
(*Exits.*)

Mme. Ranevskaya.
Now we can go. I leave with two cares weighing on me.
The first is poor old Firs. (*Glancing at her watch.*)
We still have about five minutes.

Anya.
Mamma, Firs has already been taken to the hospital.
Yasha sent him there this morning.

Mme. Ranevskaya.
My other worry is Varya. She's used to getting up
early and working; and now, with no work to do, she
is like a fish out of water. She has grown thin and
pale, and keeps crying, poor soul. (*Pause.*) You know
this very well, Yermolay Alexeyevich; I dreamed of
seeing her married to you, and it looked as though
that's how it would be. (*Whispers to* ANYA, *who nods
to* CHARLOTTA *and both go out.*) She loves you. You
find her attractive. I don't know, I don't know why
it is you seem to avoid each other; I can't understand
it.

Lopahin.

To tell you the truth, I don't understand it myself. It's all a puzzle. If there's still time, I'm ready now, at once. Let's settle it straight off, and have done with it! Without you, I feel I'll never be able to propose.

Mme. Ranevskaya.

That's splendid. After all, it will only take a minute. I'll call her at once. . . .

Lopahin.

And luckily, here's champagne, too. (*Looks at the glasses.*) Empty! Somebody's drunk it all. (*Yasha coughs.*) That's what you might call guzzling . . .

Mme. Ranevskaya.

(*Animatedly.*) Excellent! We'll go and leave you alone. Yasha, *allez!* I'll call her. (*At the door.*) Varya, leave everything and come here. Come! (*Exits with* YASHA.)

Lopahin.

(*Looking at his watch.*) Yes . . . (*Pause behind the door, smothered laughter and whispering; at last, enter* VARYA.)

Varya.

(*Looking over the luggage in leisurely fashion.*) Strange, I can't find it . . .

Lopahin.

What are you looking for?

Varya.

Packed it myself, and I don't remember . . . (*Pause.*)

Lopahin.

Where are you going now, Varya?

Varya.

I? To the Ragulins'. I've arranged to take charge there—as housekeeper, if you like.

Lopahin.

At Yashnevo? About fifty miles from here. (*Pause.*) Well, life in this house is ended!

Varya.

(*Examining luggage.*) Where is it? Perhaps I put it in the chest. Yes, life in this house is ended. . . . There will be no more of it.

Lopahin.

And I'm just off to Kharkov—by this next train. I've

a lot to do there. I'm leaving Yepihodov here ... I've taken him on.

Varya.
Oh!

Lopahin.
Last year at this time, it was snowing, if you remember, but now it's sunny and there's no wind. It's cold, though. ... It must be three below.

Varya.
I didn't look. (*Pause.*) And besides, our thermometer's broken. (*Pause. Voice from the yard:* "Yermolay Alexeyevich!")

Lopahin.
(*As if he had been waiting for the call.*) This minute! (*Exits quickly.*)

(VARYA *sits on the floor and sobs quietly, her head on a bundle of clothes. Enter* MME. RANEVSKAYA *cautiously.*)

Mme. Ranevskaya.
Well? (*Pause.*) We must be going.

Varya.
(*Wiping her eyes.*) Yes, it's time, Mamma dear. I'll be able to get to the Ragulins' today, if only we don't miss the train.

Mme. Ranevskaya.
(*At the door.*) Anya, put your things on. (*Enter* ANYA, GAYEV, CHARLOTTA. GAYEV *wears a heavy overcoat with a hood. Enter servants and coachmen.* YEPIHODOV *bustles about the luggage.*)

Mme. Ranevskaya.
Now we can start on our journey.

Anya.
(*Joyfully.*) On our journey!

Gayev.
My friends, my dear, cherished friends, leaving this house forever, can I be silent? Can I, at leave-taking, refrain from giving utterance to those emotions that now fill my being?

Anya.
(*Imploringly.*) Uncle!

Varya.
Uncle, Uncle dear, don't.

Gayev.
(*Forlornly.*) I'll bank the yellow in the side pocket
. . . I'll be silent . . .

(*Enter* TROFIMOV, *then* LOPAHIN.)

Trofimov.
Well, ladies and gentlemen, it's time to leave.
Lopahin.
Yepihodov, my coat.
Mme. Ranevskaya.
I'll sit down just a minute. It seems as though I'd
never before seen what the walls of this house were
like, the ceilings, and now I look at them hungrily,
with such tender affection.
Gayev.
I remember when I was six years old sitting on that
windowsill on Whitsunday, watching my father going
to church.
Mme. Ranevskaya.
Has everything been taken?
Lopahin.
I think so. (*Putting on his overcoat.*) Yepihodov, see
that everything's in order.
Yepihodov.
(*In a husky voice.*) You needn't worry, Yermolay
Alexeyevich.
Lopahin.
What's the matter with your voice?
Yepihodov.
I just had a drink of water. I must have swallowed
something.
Yasha.
(*Contemptuously.*) What ignorance!
Mme. Ranevskaya.
When we're gone, not a soul will be left here.
Lopahin.
Until the spring.

(VARYA *pulls an umbrella out of a bundle, as though
about to hit someone with it.* LOPAHIN *pretends to be
frightened.*)

Varya.
Come, come, I had no such idea!

Trofimov.
Ladies and gentlemen, let's get into the carriages—it's time. The train will be in directly.

Varya.
Petya, there they are, your rubbers, by that trunk. (*Tearfully.*) And what dirty old things they are!

Trofimov.
(*Puts on rubbers.*) Let's go, ladies and gentlemen.

Gayev.
(*Greatly upset, afraid of breaking down.*) The train ... the station. .... Three cushions in the side pocket, I'll bank this one in the corner ...

Mme. Ranevskaya.
Let's go.

Lopahin.
Are we all here? No one in there? (*Locks the side door on the left.*) There are some things stored here, better lock up. Let us go!

Anya.
Good-bye, old house! Good-bye, old life!

Trofimov.
Hail to you, new life!

(*Exits with* ANYA. VARYA *looks round the room and goes out slowly.* YASHA *and* CHARLOTTA *with her dog go out.*)

Lopahin.
And so, until the spring. Go along, friends ... Bye-bye! (*Exits.*)

(MME. RANEVSKAYA *and* GAYEV *remain alone. As though they had been waiting for this, they throw themselves on each other's necks, and break into subdued, restrained sobs, afraid of being overheard.*)

Gayev.
(*In despair.*) My sister! My sister!

Mme. Ranevskaya.
Oh, my orchard—my dear, sweet, beautiful orchard! My life, my youth, my happiness—good-bye! Good-bye! (*Voice of* ANYA, *gay and summoning:* "Mamma!" *Voice of* TROFIMOV, *gay and excited:* "Halloo!")

Mme. Ranevskaya.
One last look at the walls, at the windows.... Our poor mother loved to walk about this room ...

Gayev.
My sister, my sister! (*Voice of* ANYA: "Mamma!" *Voice of* TROFIMOV: "Halloo!")

Mme. Ranevskaya.
We're coming.

(*They go out. The stage is empty. The sound of doors being locked, of carriages driving away. Then silence. In the stillness is heard the muffled sound of the ax striking a tree, a mournful, lonely sound.*

Footsteps are heard. FIRS *appears in the doorway on the right. He is dressed as usual in a jacket and white waistcoat and wears slippers. He is ill.*)

Firs.
(*Goes to the door, tries the handle.*) Locked! They've gone ... (*Sits down on the sofa.*) They've forgotten me.... Never mind ... I'll sit here a bit ... I'll wager Leonid Andreyevich hasn't put his fur coat on, he's gone off in his light overcoat ... (*Sighs anxiously.*) I didn't keep an eye on him.... Ah, when they're young, they're green ... (*Mumbles something indistinguishable.*) Life has gone by as if I had never lived. (*Lies down.*) I'll lie down a while.... There's no strength left in you, old fellow; nothing is left, nothing. Ah, you addlehead! (*Lies motionless. A distant sound is heard coming from the sky, as it were, the sound of a snapping string mournfully dying away. All is still again, and nothing is heard but the strokes of the ax against a tree far away in the orchard.*)

THE BACKGROUND

by Ronald Hingley

1. THE COMPOSITION

(a) First intimations

According to Stanislavsky the idea of *The Cherry Orchard* first presented itself to Chekhov in vague form in 1901 during the period of rehearsals for the first performance of *Three Sisters* (see *Works*, 1944–51, xi, pp. 595–6). Letters from Chekhov to Olga Knipper shortly after the first performance of *Three Sisters* show that he intended to write a farce or comedy for the Moscow Art Theatre. 'The next play I write will definitely be funny, very funny—at least in intention.' (*Letter of 7 March 1901*.) 'There are moments when an overwhelming desire comes over me to write a four-act farce [водевиль] or comedy for the Art Theatre. And I shall write one if nothing prevents me, only I shan't deliver it to the theatre before the end of 1903.' (*Letter of 22 April 1901*.)

In view of Chekhov's later repeated insistence that

The Cherry Orchard was a comedy or farce, it seems likely that these early intimations have some bearing on the play. The same is true of the following passage in a letter to Olga Knipper of 20 January 1902: 'The reason I haven't written to you about my forthcoming play is not that I don't trust you, as you say in your letter, but that I don't yet trust the play. It's just a faint glimmering in the brain, like the earliest moment of the dawn, and I don't yet know myself what it's like or what will come of it, and it changes its shape every day.' Similarly Chekhov wrote to Stanislavsky about an unnamed play on 1 October 1902: 'I'll be in Moscow on 15 October and I'll explain to you why my play still isn't ready. I have a subject, but so far I haven't got steam up.'

The first recorded mention of the title *The Cherry Orchard* occurs in December 1902: 'My *Cherry Orchard* will be in three acts. That's what I think, but actually I haven't yet made up my mind definitely.' (*Letter to O. L. Knipper, 24 Dec. 1902.*) References in Chekhov's letters of January and February 1903 show that he had not yet started writing the play, but that he was turning it over in his mind. Two characters, who can be equated with Mrs. Ranevsky and Varya respectively, an 'old woman' and a 'silly girl', had occurred to him.

'I wanted to do *The Cherry Orchard* in three long acts, but I may do it in four. It makes no difference to me, because the play will be just the same anyway whether it's in three or four acts.' (*Letter to O. L. Knipper, 3 Jan. 1903.*)

'With regard to the play, I can tell you the following:

'It's true that I've thought of a play and I already have a name for it (*The Cherry Orchard,* but this is a secret for the moment), and I shall probably get down to writing it no later than the end of February, if I'm well, of course.

'The central part in this play is that of an old woman

[Mrs. Ranevsky], to the author's great regret!' (*Letter to V. F. Komissarzhevskaya, 27 Jan. 1903.*)

'I'm counting on getting down to the play after 20 February and I shall finish it by 20 March. It's already completed in my head. It's called *The Cherry Orchard*, it has four acts and in Act One cherry trees can be seen in bloom through the windows, the whole orchard a mass of white. And ladies in white dresses.' (*Letter to K. S. Stanislavsky, 5 Feb. 1903.*)

'I shall start writing the play on 21 February. You'll play the silly girl [Varya]. But who's going to play the old mother? Who indeed? We'll have to ask M. F. [Mariya Fyodorovna Andreyeva].' (*Letter to O. L. Knipper, 11 Feb. 1903.*)

'Your part is a complete fool of a girl. Do you want to play a silly girl [Varya]? A kind-hearted simpleton.' (*Letter to O. L. Knipper, 22 Feb. 1903.*)

(*b*) *First phase of writing, March–April 1903*

Chekhov started writing *The Cherry Orchard* in March 1903. 'I've laid out the paper for the play and written down the title.' (*Letter to O. L. Knipper, 1 March 1903.*) During March and the first half of April he worked on the play, breaking off in mid-April to visit Moscow and St. Petersburg.

'If the play doesn't work out the way I've planned it, you must punch my head. There's a comic part [Lopakhin] for Stanislavsky, and one for you too.' (*Letter to O. L. Knipper, 5 and 6 March 1903.*)

'Incidentally, I'm not getting on all that well with the play. One of the main parts isn't sufficiently worked out yet and is causing trouble. But I think the character will be clear by Easter and I shall be out of the wood.' (*Letter to O. L. Knipper, 18 March 1903.*)

'There will be a *Cherry Orchard* and I shall try to

have as few characters as possible, that makes it more intimate.' (*Letter to O. L. Knipper, 21 March 1903.*)

'Will you [the Moscow Art Theatre] have an actress for the part of the elderly lady in *The Cherry Orchard*? If not there won't even be any play, I won't even write it.' (*Letter to O. L. Knipper, 11 April 1903.*)

'I don't very much want to write for your theatre [the Moscow Art Theatre], mainly because you haven't got an old woman. They'll start trying to foist the part of the old woman [Mrs. Ranevsky] on you, but there's another part for you and anyway you've already played an old lady in *The Seagull*.' (*Letter to O. L. Knipper, 15 April 1903.*)

'The play is coming on bit by bit, but I'm afraid I've rather lost my touch.' (*Letter to O. L. Knipper, 17 April 1903.*)

(c) *Second phase of writing, July–October 1903*

On returning to Yalta in July 1903, Chekhov resumed work on *The Cherry Orchard*. The following quotations from his letters record progress from then to mid-October, when he sent the completed draft to the Moscow Art Theatre.

'My play isn't ready. It's moving rather sluggishly, which I put down to laziness, the marvellous weather and the difficulty of the subject. When the play is ready, or before it's ready, I'll write to you or better still send a telegram. Your part [Lopakhin] has come off quite well, I think, though actually I don't take it upon myself to judge, for I understand precious little about plays in general when I read them.' (*Letter to K. S. Stanislavsky, 28 July 1903.*)

'Now, as regards my . . . play *The Cherry Orchard*, everything's fine so far. I'm getting on with the work bit by bit. Even if I am a bit late with it, it won't matter all that much. I've reduced the décor side of the play to the minimum, no special sets will be needed and no special displays of ingenuity required.

'In Act Two of my play I've substituted an old chapel and a well for the river. It's more peaceful that way. Only in Act Two you must give me some proper green fields and a road and a sense of distance unusual on the stage.' (*Letter to V. I. Nemirovich-Danchenko, 22 Aug. 1903.*)

'My play (if I carry on working as I've worked until today) will be finished soon, don't worry. Writing Act Two was difficult, very much so, but I think it's turned out all right. I shall call the play a comedy.

'Olga [Knipper] will take the part of the mother in my play. But who's going to play the daughter aged seventeen or eighteen, a slender young girl, I don't take it upon myself to decide. Anyway, we'll see about that when the time comes.' (*Letter to V. I. Nemirovich-Danchenko, 2 Sept. 1903.*)

'Dear Mariya Petrovna, don't believe what anyone says. Not a single living soul has read my play yet. The part I've written for you [Varya] isn't that of a "prig", but of a very charming girl with whom you, or so I hope, will be quite satisfied. I've almost finished the play, but fell ill just over a week ago, started coughing and became very weak. In fact it was as if last year's business had started again. Now, i.e. today, it's warm and my health seems to have got better, but I still can't write because I have a headache. Olga [Knipper] won't bring the play with her, I'll send all four acts as soon as I have the chance to get down to it again for a whole day. It hasn't turned out as a drama, but as a comedy, in places even a farce, and I'm afraid I may get into hot water with Vladimir Ivanovich [Nemirovich-Danchenko]. Konstantin Sergeyevich [Stanislavsky] has a big part. There aren't many parts altogether.' (*Letter to M. P. Alekseyeva [Lilina], 15 Sept. 1903.*)

'My splendid little wife, I feel a bit more comfortable today. Obviously I'm getting back to normal. I can look at my manuscript without being angry now, I'm writing already, and when I've finished I'll send you a telegram at once. The last act will be gay. Actually the whole play is gay and frivolous.' (*Letter to O. L. Knipper, 21 Sept. 1903.*)

'Act Four of my play will be thin in content compared with the other acts, but effective. The end of your part seems not bad to me. In general don't be down-hearted. Everything's fine.

'My regards to Vishnevsky, and tell him to stock up with gentleness and elegance for a part [Gayev] in my play.' (*Letter to O. L. Knipper, 23 Sept. 1903.*)

'You'll probably get this letter after you've had my telegram about finishing the play. Act Four is proving easy to write, it all seems to go very smoothly, and if I haven't finished it quickly it's because I keep falling ill.

'However boring my play may be, I think there's something new about it. Incidentally, there's not a single pistol shot in the whole play. There's a good part [Trofimov] for Kachalov. Do keep an eye open for someone to play the seventeen-year-old girl and write to me about it.' (*Letter to O. L. Knipper, 25 Sept. 1903.*)

'My darling little horse, I've already sent you a telegram telling you the play's finished and all four acts are written. I'm already copying it. It's true that my characters have turned out as living people, but what the play is like as a play I don't know. When I send it you'll read it and find out.' (*Letter to O. L. Knipper, 27 Sept. 1903.*)

'The play's finished already, but I'm copying it slowly as I have to revise it and rethink it. I'll just send two or three passages unfinished, I'm putting them off till later. You must excuse me. . . .

'Oh, if only you could take the part of the governess

in my play! It's the best part. I don't like the others.'
(*Letter to O. L. Knipper, 29 Sept. 1903.*)

'I write every day. Only a bit maybe, but I still do
write. When I send the play you'll read it and see what
might have been made out of the subject under favourable circumstances—that is, given good health. As it is
the whole thing is quite disgusting, you write a couple
of lines a day and get used to what's been written etc.
etc.' (*Letter to O. L. Knipper, 2 Oct. 1903.*)

'My play is moving, and I'm finishing copying Act
Three today and starting Act Four. Act Three is the
least boring, but the second act is as boring and as
monotonous as a cobweb.

'Who, oh who, will play my governess?' (*Letter to
O. L. Knipper, 8 Oct. 1903.*)

'I'm in splendid form. I'm copying the play and I'll
soon be finished, darling, I swear it. When I send it
off I'll let you have a telegram. I assure you that every
extra day is only to the good, for my play is getting
better and better and the characters are now quite clear.
Only I'm afraid there are passages which the censor
may strike out. That will be terrible.' (*Letter to O. L.
Knipper, 9 Oct. 1903.*)

'The play's finished now, finally finished, and tomorrow evening, or at the latest on the morning of the 14th,
will be sent to Moscow. At the same time I'll send you
one or two comments. If any alterations are needed I
think they'll be very small ones. The worst thing about
the play is that I didn't write it at a sitting, but spent a
long, long time over it, so it's bound to seem a bit spun
out. Anyway, we'll see what happens.' (*Letter to O. L.
Knipper, 12 Oct. 1903.*)

2. THE TEXT

(a) Alterations imposed by the censorship

The Cherry Orchard was submitted to the theatrical censorship in November 1903 and objection was taken to two passages in Act Two. In place of these passages Chekhov supplied alternative versions, inserted in the manuscript in his handwriting. The offending passages were enclosed in brackets in the manuscript, but were not crossed out. The two passages are as follows:

(i) *Restored original text as translated by Roland Hingley* (see Trofimov's speech, p. 59, above):

. . . everyone knows the workers are abominably fed and sleep without proper bedding, thirty or forty to a room—with bed-bugs everywhere, to say nothing of the stench, the damp, the moral degradation.

Alternative version supplied by Chekhov and incorporated in the 1904 editions, p. 59, above:

. . . the vast majority of us, ninety-nine out of a hundred, live like savages. At the least provocation—a punch in the jaw and curses. They eat disgustingly, sleep in filth and stuffiness. . . .

(ii) *Restored original text as translated by Roland Hingley* (see Trofimov's speech, p. 63, above):

Owning living souls, that's what has changed you all so completely, those who went before and those alive today, so that your mother, you yourself, your uncle—you don't realize that you're actually living on credit. You're living on other people, the very people you won't even let inside your own front door.

Alternative version supplied by Chekhov and incorporated in the 1904 editions, p. 63, above:

Oh, it's terrifying! Your orchard is a fearful place, and when you pass through it in the evening or at night, the old bark on the trees gleams faintly, and the cherry trees seem to be dreaming of things that happened a hundred, two hundred years ago and to be tormented by painful visions.

(*b*) *Alterations made in the Lenin Library manuscript*

The manuscript preserved in the Lenin Library contains some insertions and alterations made by Chekhov at points where an earlier, rejected version remains legible. Among these the following involve the only alterations of significance:

(i) *In Act One, in Lopakhin's speech (p. 36), the present text from* 'I feel I want to tell you something very pleasant' *to* 'Here is my plan' *was inserted in the manuscript in place of the following earlier version:*

Only I just want to tell you before I go. [*Looks at his watch.*] It's about the estate, just a couple of words. I want to offer you a means of escape. To stop your estate running at a loss you must get up at four o'clock in the morning every day and work all day. For you of course this is impossible, I can see that. But there is another way out. Listen to me.

(ii) *The following exchange, which appears in the manuscript after* 'ANYA. There goes Yepikhodov' (*see p. 60), was cut out of the final version:*

Varya.
Why do we have him in the house? He only eats all the time and drinks tea all day.
Lopakhin.
And he's preparing to shoot himself.
Mme. Ranevskaya.
But I like Yepikhodov. When he talks about his misfortunes it's really funny. Don't give him his notice, Varya.

Varya.
I must, Mother. He must be dismissed, the worthless fellow.

(c) Variants found in the Lenin Library manuscript

The following are some of the variants found in the Lenin Library manuscript and superseded in the final version:

(i) *Act One*. Minor alterations only are involved, and include the removal of one of Charlotte's 'tricks' (see p. 40).

In the final version Charlotte's words 'I don't see the need. I want to sleep' *were substituted for the following speech, found in the manuscript:*

Charlotte.
(*Going up to the door*.) Someone's standing behind the door. Who's there? (*There is a knock on the other side of the door*.) Who's that knocking? (*A knock*.) That's the gentleman to whom I'm engaged.

(ii) *Act Two*. It was in Act Two that the most extensive alterations were made.

1. *In the manuscript Charlotte does not appear at all at the beginning of the act, which continues as follows after the words* 'The sun will soon be setting' (*see p. 49*):

(YASHA *and* DUNYASHA *are sitting on the bench.* YEPIKHODOV *stands near them.* TROFIMOV *and* ANYA *pass by on the road from the estate.*)

Anya.
Our great-aunt is lonely and very rich. She doesn't like Mother. During my first few days at her house I was in low spirits and she talked to me very little. It was all right later and she laughed. She promised to send some money and gave me and Charlotte some for the journey. But what an eerie sensation. How depressing to feel oneself a poor relation.

Trofimov.
I think there's someone here already, someone sitting here. In that case let's go on a bit further.

Anya.
I've been away from home for three weeks. How I've missed it.

(*They go off.*)

The manuscript then continues as the final version with 'DUNYASHA (*to* YASHA.) How wonderful it must be though to have stayed abroad!' (*see p. 50*).

2. *The following passage, which was cut out of the final version, appears in the manuscript after* 'MRS. RANEVSKY. Perhaps we shall think of something' (*see p. 54*):

(VARYA *and* CHARLOTTE *pass along the road from the estate.* CHARLOTTE *is wearing man's clothing and carries a gun.*)

Varya.
She's an intelligent girl and well brought up, and nothing can happen to her. Still, it's not right for her to be left alone with a young man. Supper's at nine o'clock, Charlotte. Mind you're not late.

Charlotte.
I'm not hungry. (*Quietly sings a song.*)

Varya.
That's not important. You must have some as a matter of form. Look, you see—they're sitting there on the bank.

(VARYA *and* CHARLOTTE *go off.*)

3. Act Two has a different ending in the manuscript from that in the final version. It includes some of the material given to Charlotte at the beginning of the act in the final version.

In the manuscript the end of Act Two, after Anya's

speech (*p. 64*) 'How well you put that', *reads as follows:*

Trofimov.
Sh! There's somebody coming. Varya's at it again. (*Angrily.*) She really is infuriating.

Anya.
Oh well, let's go down to the river. It's lovely there.

Trofimov.
Come on then.

Anya.
The moon will soon be up. (*They go off.*)

(*Enter* FIRS *followed by* CHARLOTTE. FIRS, *muttering, looks for something on the ground near the bench and lights a match.*)

Firs.
(*Mutters.*) Oh, get away with you, you nincompoop!

Charlotte.
(*Sits on the bench, and removes her peaked cap.*) Is that you, Firs? What are you looking for?

Firs.
The mistress has lost her purse.

Charlotte.
(*Helping him to look.*) Here's a fan. And here's a handkerchief. It smells of scent. (*Pause.*) There's nothing else. Mrs. Ranevsky's forever losing things. She's thrown away her life as well. (*Quietly sings a song.*) I haven't any proper identification papers, old man, I don't know how old I am and I think of myself as a little girl. (*Puts her cap on* FIRS'S *head. He sits there without moving.*) Oh, I love you, my dear old gentleman. (*Laughs.*) *Eins, zwei, drei!* (*Takes the cap off* FIRS'S *head and puts it on her own.*) When I was little, Father and Mother used to go on tour round all the fairs giving performances.

[*The passage continues almost exactly as on pp. 49– 50 down to* 'I don't know a thing', *after which it continues as follows:*]

Firs.
When I was about twenty or twenty-five, I was walk-

ing along with the son of our priest and Vasily the cook, and there was a man sitting on the stone right here in this very spot—no one from these parts, a stranger. I was scared for some reason and went away, and after I'd gone the two of them went and killed him—he had some money.

Charlotte.

Well then? *Weiter!*

Firs.

Well, then the legal people turned up, started asking questions. They ran them in and me along with them. I spent a couple of years in prison. It was all right after that, they let me out. Ages ago, it was. (*Pause.*) You can't remember everything.

Charlotte.

It's time you were dead, Granddad. (*Eats a gherkin.*)

Firs.

Eh? (*Mutters to himself.*) So then we all drove off together and then we got held up. The old chap jumped off the cart, picked up a sack. And inside that sack there was another sack. He looks at it and then something suddenly gives a jerk, jerk, jerk!

Charlotte.

(*Laughing, quietly.*) A jerk, jerk, jerk! (*Carries on eating the gherkin.*)

(*Someone is heard walking quietly along the road and quietly playing a balalaika. The moon rises. Somewhere near the poplars* VARYA *is looking for* ANYA *and calling:* 'Anya! Where are you?')

Note on the alterations to Act Two. The 'supplementary' manuscript. The alterations to Act Two, made after the play had been passed by the censorship, were so extensive that they had to be submitted for supplementary censorship. The text of the relevant passages in Chekhov's handwriting (the 'supplementary' manuscript) is preserved in the archives of the Moscow Art Theatre Museum. It has been published in *Literaturnoye nasledstvo: Chekhov*, pp. 141–6, with an introductory note by A. R. Vladimirskaya. A comparison of the text in this supplementary manuscript with that of the final version reveals a number of minor variants of interest to students of Chekhov's technique of revision, but the individual variants are not of sufficient substance to call for translation.

(iii) *Acts Three and Four*. Only a few minor alterations are involved, including the following:

1. *In Act Three* (*see p. 77*) *the stage direction* 'Swings the stick just as LOPAKHIN *enters*' *reads as follows in the manuscript:*

(*The blow strikes* LOPAKHIN, *who comes in at that moment.*)

2. *The passage* (*see p. 83*) *from* 'Never mind' *to* 'a fine, delicate soul' *is not in the mauscript and was inserted in the final version.*

3. SOME FURTHER COMMENTS BY CHEKHOV

(a) *From October 1903 to the first performance*

Between mid-October 1903, when Chekhov sent the completed *Cherry Orchard* to the Moscow Art Theatre, and 17 January 1904, when the first performance took place, the play remained his constant preoccupation. This is shown by the following comments from his letters and elsewhere, made during the period and dealing in detail with problems of interpretation and casting. The letters tail off at the end of November because Chekhov left for Moscow on 2 December, and was able to be present at rehearsals of *The Cherry Orchard* at the Moscow Art Theatre.

'You will play Lyuba Ranevsky since there's nobody else to. She's not dressed luxuriously, but with great taste. She's intelligent, very kind and absent-minded. She's nice to everybody and always has a smile on her face.

'Anya absolutely must be played by a young actress. . . .

'Gayev is for Vishnevsky. Ask Vishnevsky to listen to people playing billiards and write down as many billiard terms as possible. I don't play billiards, or rather I did play at one time and have forgotten all about it now, and everything about it in the play is haphazard. I'll settle the thing with Vishnevsky later on and make the necessary insertions. . . .

'Charlotte—a question mark. I'll put in some more lines for her in Act Four—yesterday I had a stomach-ache when I was copying Act Four and couldn't make any new insertions. In Act Four Charlotte plays a trick with Trofimov's galoshes. Rayevskaya won't be able to play it. What we need here is an actress with a sense of humour. . . .

'I must admit I'm terribly bored with the play. If anything about it isn't clear, write and tell me.

'It's an old manor house. At one time people lived there in great style and this must be conveyed by the set. There is an atmosphere of riches and comfort.

'Varya's a bit crude and a bit stupid, but very kindhearted.' (*Letter to O. L. Knipper, 14 Oct. 1903.*)

'I must revise and polish off a few odd things about the play. I don't think it'll take more than a quarter of an hour. Act Four hasn't received its final polish, I must move one or two things around in Act Two and perhaps change two or three words at the end of Act Three. As it is, it's perhaps like the end of *Uncle Vanya.*' (*Letter to O. L. Knipper, 17 Oct. 1903.*)

'The thing that frightened me most was the sluggishness of Act Two and a certain unfinished quality about the student Trofimov. You see, Trofimov is in exile off and on and gets chucked out of the university every so often, and how is one to depict that kind of thing?' (*Letter to O. L. Knipper, 19 Oct. 1903.*)

'I had a telegram from Stanislavsky today in which

he calls my play a work of genius, which is to over-
praise the play and rob it of a good half of the success
which it might achieve under favourable conditions.
Nemirovich hasn't yet sent me a list of the actors who
are taking part in the play, but I'm still scared. He's
already sent me a telegram saying that Anya resembles
Irina [in *Three Sisters*]. . . . But Anya's about as much
like Irina as I'm like Burdzhalov [an actor and producer
at the Art Theatre]. Anya is above all a child who remains gay right up to the end, doesn't know life and
never cries except in Act Two, where she only has tears
in her eyes. But, you know, M. F. [Andreyeva] will
make the whole part into one long whine, and what's
more she's too old. Who's playing Charlotte?' (*Letter to
O. L. Knipper, 21 Oct. 1903.*)

'You write that Vishnevsky can't play Gayev. Then
who can? Stanislavsky? In that case who's to play
Lopakhin? It can't be given to Luzhsky on any account,
he'll either make a very colourless job of it or ham it.
He must play Yepikhodov. No, don't you be too hard on
Vishnevsky.

'Nemirovich writes that there are lots of tears in my
play and some crudities. Darling, write and tell me what
you find to be wrong and what people are saying, and
I'll change it. It's not too late, after all, I can still revise
a whole act.

'So the actors have taken to Pishchik, have they? I'm
delighted.' (*Letter to O. L. Knipper, 23 Oct. 1903.*)

'I'd very much like to look in on rehearsals. I'm
afraid Anya might be a bit weepy (for some reason you
find her similar to Irina) and I'm afraid of her being
played by an actress who isn't young. Anya doesn't cry
once in my text, she nowhere talks in a weepy tone of
voice. She does have tears in her eyes in Act Two, but
the mood is gay and lively. What's this in your telegram
about the play being full of people crying? Where are
they? Varya's the only one, but that's because Varya's
a cry-baby by nature, and her tears shouldn't depress

the audience. You'll often find the stage-direction "through tears" in my text, but that only shows the mood of the characters and not their tears. There isn't a cemetery in Act Two.' (*Letter to V. I. Nemirovich-Danchenko, 23 Oct. 1903.*)

'My darling little horse, what's the point of translating my play into French? Why, it's a mad idea. The French won't understand anything about Yermolay [Lopakhin] or about the sale of the estate and will only be bored. It's a bad idea, darling, there's no point in it.' (*Letter to O. L. Knipper, 24 Oct. 1903.*)

'No, I never wanted to make Mrs. Ranevsky a person who has calmed down. Nothing less than death can calm a woman like that. But perhaps I don't understand what you mean. It's not hard to play Ranevsky. It's only necessary to strike the right note from the very beginning. It's necessary to invent a smile and a way of smiling, and it's necessary to know how to dress. Anyway, you'll manage all that with a little good will and good health.' (*Letter to O. L. Knipper, 25 Oct. 1903.*)

'If Mariya Petrovna [Lilina] would agree to play Charlotte, what could be better than that? I had it in mind, but didn't dare say so. The fact that she's frail and short doesn't matter, she's too old for Anya. . . . Konstantin Sergeyevich [Stanislavsky] and no one else must play the merchant [Lopakhin]. After all, he's not a merchant in the vulgar sense of the word, that must be borne in mind.' (*Letter to O. L. Knipper, 28 Oct. 1903.*)

'Stanislavsky will make a most excellent and original Gayev, but in that case who's to play Lopakhin? After all, the part of Lopakhin is the central one. If it doesn't come off the whole play will be a flop. Lopakhin mustn't be played by anyone rowdy, and he doesn't inevitably have to be a [typical] merchant. He's a gentle person.' (*Letter to O. L. Knipper, 30 Oct. 1903.*)

'Many thanks for your letter and thanks for your telegram too. Letters are very precious to me now, firstly
because I'm stuck here on my own and, secondly, I sent
off the play three weeks ago and I only had your letter
yesterday. If it hadn't been for my wife I wouldn't have
known a thing, and heaven knows what I might have
imagined. When I wrote the part of Lopakhin I thought
of it as your part. If you don't like the look of it for
some reason, then take Gayev. True, Lopakhin is a
merchant, but he's a decent person in the full sense of
the words and his bearing must be that of a completely
dignified and intelligent man. There must be nothing
petty about him, no tricks, and my idea was that you'd
make a brilliant success of this part, which is the central
one in the play. If you take Gayev, give Lopakhin to
Vishnevsky. He won't make an artistic Lopakhin, but at
least he won't be a petty one. Luzhsky would be only a
cold foreigner in this part. Leonidov would make a typical profiteering peasant [кулачок] of him. When
choosing an actor for this part it must not be forgotten
that Lopakhin was loved by Varya, a serious and re-
ligious girl. She wouldn't love some wretched money-
grubbing peasant.' (*Letter to K. S. Stanislavsky, 30
Oct. 1903.*)

'I don't know why Mariya Petrovna [Lilina] is so
keen on playing Anya. After all it's a short part and not
a very interesting one. My idea is that Varya suits her
much better. Nemirovich writes that she's afraid of the
resemblance between Varya and Sonya in *Uncle Vanya*.
But what resemblance is there? Varya's a nun, a silly
girl.' (*Letter to O. L. Knipper, 1 Nov. 1903.*)

'Anya can be played by anyone you like, a completely
unknown actress even, as long as she's young and looks
like a little girl and talks in a young, ringing voice. This
isn't one of the important parts.

'Varya is a more serious part—that is, if Mariya
Petrovna [Lilina] should take it. Without M.P. this part
will turn out flat and crude, and it will be necessary

to revise it and tone it down. Mariya Petrovna is unable to repeat herself, firstly because she's a talented person, and secondly because Varya does not resemble Sonya and Natasha. She's a figure in a black dress, a nun, a silly girl, a cry-baby, etc. etc.

'Gayev and Lopakhin—let Konstantin Sergeyevich [Stanislavsky] choose between these parts and try them out. If he should pick Lopakhin and succeed in this role the play would succeed. You see, if Lopakhin's colourless and is played by a colourless actor both the part and the play will fail. . . .

'Charlotte is an important part. . . . This is the part for Miss Knipper.[1] . . .

'The stationmaster who declaims *The Sinful Woman* in Act Three should be an actor with a bass voice.

'Charlotte talks good—not broken—Russian. Only she occasionally mixes up hard and soft consonants at the end of a word and confuses adjectives of the masculine and feminine gender. Pishchik is a Russian, an old man crippled with gout, old age and good living. He is stout and is dressed in a peasant's sleeveless coat . . . with heelless high boots. Lopakhin has a white waistcoat and brown boots, he waves his arms about as he walks, takes long strides and meditates while walking about—walking in a straight line. His hair isn't short and so he often throws back his head. He absent-mindedly combs his beard from back to front—i.e. from his neck in the direction of his mouth. Trofimov's quite clear, I think. Varya wears a black dress with a broad belt.

'I spent three years preparing to write *The Cherry Orchard* and for three years I've been telling you to engage an actress for the part of Lyuba Ranevsky. So don't complain if you now find yourselves playing a game of patience which just won't come out.' (*Letter to V. I. Nemirovich-Danchenko, 2 Nov. 1903.*)

'The house in the play has two stories and is large.

---

[1] Olga Knipper in fact took the part of Mrs. Ranevsky.

After all there is a mention in Act Three of a staircase going downstairs.

'The house must be large and solid. Whether it's made of wood . . . or stone, that doesn't matter. It's very old and large. Summer holiday-makers don't rent that kind of house. That kind of house is usually pulled down and the material is used to build summer cottages. The furniture is old-fashioned, of good style, and solid. The furniture and fittings haven't been affected by financial ruin and debts.

'When people buy a house of this kind they argue as follows: it's cheaper and easier to build a smaller new one than to repair this old one.' (*Letter to K. S. Stanislavsky, 5 Nov. 1903.*)

'Nemirovich sent me an express telegram asking me to reply by express telegram. Who, he asks, is to play Charlotte, Anya and Varya? There were three names opposite Varya, two unknown ones and Andreyeva. I had to choose Andreyeva. Very cunningly rigged.' (*Letter to O. L. Knipper, 7 Nov. 1903.*)

'Tell her [Muratova] to be funny in the part of Charlotte, that's the main thing. I doubt whether Lilina will succeed with Anya, she'll just be an old-fashioned girl with a squeaky voice and no more.' (*Letter to O. L. Knipper, 8 Nov. 1903.*)

'Of course you can use the same set for Acts Three and Four, the one with a hall and staircase. In general please don't stint yourself with the scenery—I defer to you. In your theatre I'm always stunned and usually sit with my mouth wide open. There's nothing more to be said about this. Whatever you do will be splendid, a hundred times better than anything I could think of.

'Dunyasha and Yepikhodov stand in the presence of Lopakhin, they don't sit down. After all, Lopakhin is very much at his ease, behaves like a squire and calls the servants "thou", while they call him "you".' (*Letter to K. S. Stanislavsky, 10 Nov. 1903.*)

'I've received the plan of Act One. The house will have two stories, which means that the garden-room also has two stories. But you know, there won't be much sunlight in the little patio formed by this garden-room, and cherries wouldn't grow there.' (*Letter to O. L. Knipper, 20 Nov. 1903.*)

'Haymaking usually takes place between 20 and 25 June, at which time I think the corncrake no longer cries, and frogs also are silent at this time of year. Only the golden oriole sings then. There isn't a cemetery. There *was* one a long time ago. Two or three grave-stones lying around any old how, that's all that's left. The bridge is a very good idea. If you can show a train without any noise, without a single sound, then carry on. I haven't anything against a single set for Acts Three and Four as long as the entrances and exits are con-venient in Act Four.' (*Letter to K. S. Stanislavsky, 23 Nov. 1903.*)

'Konstantin Sergeyevich [Stanislavsky] wants to bring on a train in Act Two, but I think he must be re-strained. He also wants frogs and corncrakes.' (*Letter to O. L. Knipper, 23 Nov. 1903.*)

'I'm deeply convinced that my *Cherry Orchard* doesn't suit you at all. The central female part in this play is that of an old woman bound up with the past, who has nothing to do with the present, and the other parts, at least the women's, are rather petty and crude and not interesting for you.' (*Letter to V. F. Komissar-zhevskaya, 6 Jan. 1904.*)

'I think my play will be performed on 17 January. I don't expect any particular success, things are pretty slack.' (*Letter to V. K. Kharkeyevich, 13 Jan. 1904.*)

'He [Chekhov] told me that Lopakhin must look like a cross between a merchant and a professor of medicine at Moscow University. Later at rehearsal, after Act Three, he said to me: "Listen, Lopakhin doesn't shout.

He's a rich man, and rich men never shout." ' (*The actor L. M. Leonidov, quoted in 'Chekhov i teatr', p. 351.*)

(b) After the first performance

The comments made by Chekhov between the first performance of *The Cherry Orchard* on 17 January 1904 and his death in July of the same year are dispirited, frustrated, and often irritable in tone. Evidently he was dissatisfied with the interpretation of his play by the Moscow Art Theatre, but the state of his health during the months shortly before his death no doubt coloured his comments.

'My play was put on yesterday, so I'm not feeling too good. I want to slip off somewhere and I'll probably go to France by February, or at least to the Crimea.' (*Letter to I. L. Leontyev, 18 Jan. 1904.*)

'If you arrive at carnival time, that's fine. Only as far as I can see, it will be carnival time at least before our actors come to themselves and start playing *The Cherry Orchard* less confusedly and flamboyantly than now.' (*Letter to F. D. Batyushkov, 19 Jan. 1904.*)

'*The Seagull* and *Three Sisters* have long ago been translated into German (I haven't had a single farthing from them), and *The Cherry Orchard* is already being translated for Berlin and Vienna, and it won't come off there at all as they haven't got billiards, Lopakhins or students *à la* Trofimov.' (*Letter to O. L. Knipper, 4 March 1904.*)

'Tell Nemirovich that the sound in Acts Two and Four of *The Cherry Orchard* must be shorter, a lot shorter, and must be felt as coming from a great distance. What a lot of fuss about nothing—not being able to cope with a trifle like this, a mere noise, although it's so clearly described in the play.' (*Letter to O. L. Knipper, 18 March 1904.*)

'Tell the actress who plays the maid Dunyasha to read *The Cherry Orchard* in the *Znaniye* edition or in proof. Then she'll be able to see where she has to powder her face etc. etc. Do make sure she reads it. In your notebooks the whole thing's a complete mess.' (*Letter to O. L. Knipper, 24 March 1904.*)

'Lulu and K. L. [relatives of O. L. Knipper] saw *The Cherry Orchard* in March. Both of them say that Stanislavsky [as Gayev] plays repulsively in Act Four and drags things out most painfully. This is really dreadful! An act which ought to last for a maximum of twelve minutes—you're dragging it out for forty. The only thing I can say is that Stanislavsky has ruined my play. Oh, well, the less said about him the better.' (*Letter to O. L. Knipper, 29 March 1904.*)

'Why do they so obstinately call my play a "drama" in play-bills and newspaper advertisements? What Nemirovich and Stanislavsky see in my play definitely isn't what I wrote and I'm ready to swear anything you like that neither of them has read through my play carefully once. I'm sorry to say so, but I assure you I'm right.' (*Letter to O. L. Knipper, 10 April 1904.*)

4. CONTEMPORARY RECEPTION

Whether by accident or design, the first performance of *The Cherry Orchard* had been fixed for 17 January 1904, which was Chekhov's name-day and birthday. That this might well be the last birthday of Chekhov's life was a thought which nobody liked to put into words, but which could not help occurring to all who saw him in his present utterly exhausted and emaciated condition. His friends in the Art Theatre decided to take what might be their last opportunity to express their love and admiration by making the première of *The Cherry Orchard* the occasion for a public celebration in his honour. The pretext was the twenty-fifth anniversary of his début as a writer, although this particular date was at least a year premature.

An impressive programme of speeches and presentations was arranged to take place in the interval between the third and fourth acts of the play, and a large number of prominent people, representing literary, theatrical and learned associations, arrived with gifts in their hands and the manuscripts of speeches in their pockets. *The Cherry Orchard* was well under way when a startling discovery was made. Chekhov was not in the theatre! The reason for his absence was not only ill-health. He had always been embarrassed to the point of genuine suffering by official honours, even when the recipients were other people. 'They spent twenty years running a man down,' he once told Bunin when discussing jubilee celebrations, 'and then present him with an aluminum goose-quill pen, and spend a whole day churning out solemn clap-trap to the accompaniment of kisses and tears.' Now that his own turn had come he simply could not face it, and his friends almost had to use force to make him leave his lodgings.

The third act was finishing when he reached the theatre. Pale and weak, he took up his position on the stage and the applause which broke out was such as to leave him in no doubt of the place which he held in the affections of the audience. It is difficult for anyone except a Russian to appreciate the warm personal feeling with which he was greeted that night by people who, although many of them had never seen him before, knew and loved him for his writings, and who, moreover, still had the words of *The Cherry Orchard* ringing in their ears.

He had hardly taken his place on the stage when he was seized by a fit of uncontrollable coughing. People in the audience began to shout, 'Sit down, Anton Pavlovich', 'A chair for Anton Pavlovich', but he insisted on remaining on his feet. The speeches and presentations began. There was an address on behalf of the Lovers of Russian Literature by Professor A. N.

Veselovsky, and another on behalf of the Moscow Little Theatre by the actress Fedotova. There were many other speeches, including some by representatives of the liberal press in which Chekhov had published much of his best work. Finally Nemirovich-Danchenko rounded things off with an eloquent tribute in which he expressed what all his colleagues in the Art Theatre felt: 'Our theatre is so much indebted to your talent, to your tender heart and pure soul, that you have every right to say "This is my theatre".'

Knowing that his friends and admirers were sincerely trying to please him, Chekhov listened with great attention and seriousness. All the same there were times when those who knew him best caught a glint of ironical humour in his expression. One of these points occurred when a new speaker began his oration with the words 'Dear and most honoured Anton Pavlovich'. Stanislavsky, who, as Gayev in *The Cherry Orchard,* had to deliver a speech to an old book-case beginning 'Dear and most honoured book-case', caught Chekhov's eye at this moment. The exchange of glances showed him that Chekhov was as much amused by the coincidence as he was.

Despite the personal acclaim which Chekhov received at the first performance of *The Cherry Orchard,* it was some time, according to Nemirovich-Danchenko, before the play really 'got through to its audience' (*Works, 1944–51, xi, p. 605*). Contemporary reviews tended to dwell on the social commentary contained in the play. Dissatisfaction was expressed with certain characters, especially with Trofimov (for being too vague a representative of the rising generation) and with Lopakhin, who was found surprising because he did not conform with preconceived ideas about the typical Russian merchant.

A VISIT TO FRIENDS

A Story
by Chekhov

Translated by I. C. Chertok and Jean Gardner

A letter came one morning:

MY DEAR MISHA,
   You have utterly forgotten us; do come and pay us a visit right away. We are longing to see you. We both beseech you on our knees, come today, let us see your bright eyes. We are waiting impatiently.

                                                    TA and VA.
   KUZMINKY, June 7

   The letter was from Tatyana Alexeyevna Losev who ten or twelve years ago, when Podgorin was living at Kuzminky, used to be called Ta, for short. But who was this Va? Long conversations came back to Podgorin—happy laughter, novels, strolls in the evening, and a whole flower garden of girls and young women who were living in and around Kuzminky then. And he remembered a simple, lively, intelligent face with freckles that went well with the dark red hair—this was Varya, or Varvara Pavlovna, Tatyana's close friend. She had finished her medical studies and was working in a factory somewhere the other side of Tula, and now, evidently, she had arrived in Kuzminky as a guest.
   Darling Va! thought Podgorin, giving himself up to memories. What a wonderful girl!

Tatyana, Varya and he were almost the same age, but he had been a student then, while they were already grown-up girls, old enough to be married, and they looked upon him as a little boy. And although he was a lawyer now and beginning to go gray, they still called him Misha, thought of him as a very young man and said that he had had no experience of life yet.

He was very fond of them, but seemed fonder of them in retrospect than in reality. The present state of affairs was unfamiliar to him, difficult to understand and strange. And this short, playful letter was strange too, a letter they had probably spent a long time composing, with effort, and Tatyana's husband, Sergei Sergeyich, had probably been standing right behind her as she wrote . . . Kuzminky had come to her as a dowry only six years ago, but it had already been ruined by this same Sergei Sergeyich. And now whenever the time came to settle accounts with the bank or to make a payment on the mortgages, they turned to Podgorin, as a lawyer, for advice, and on top of that they had already asked him twice for loans. This time, too, they obviously wanted either advice or money from him.

He no longer felt drawn to Kuzminky as in former days. It was cheerless there. There was no longer any laughter, or hubbub, or happy carefree faces, or secret meetings on quiet moonlit nights—but above all there was no longer youth; and it was all enchanting, probably, in memory only. . . . Besides Ta and Va, there was also Na, Tatyana's sister Nadezhda, whom they referred to, either in jest or in earnest, as his fiancée. She had grown up under his very eyes; they had expected him to marry her, and at one time he had been in love with her and intended proposing to her—but here she was, already twenty-five and still he had not married her . . .

Strange how it all came about, he was thinking now, as he reread the letter with discomfiture. But I can't possibly *not* go, they would be hurt.

The fact that he had not visited the Losevs for a long time lay heavy on his conscience. And after he had walked up and down his room thinking things over, he forced himself to a decision and resolved to go and stay with them for two or three days, fulfill his obligation and afterward feel free and at peace with himself, at least until next summer. He told his servants, as he was getting ready to leave for the Brest railway station after breakfast, that he would be back in three days.

It was a two-hour ride from Moscow to Kuzminky, and after that twenty minutes by horse from the station. From the station one could see Tatyana's woodlands and three tall narrow summer cottages which Losev had begun to build but never finished, having embarked on various questionable transactions in the first years after his marriage. These summer cottages had ruined him, along with sundry other business ventures and frequent trips to Moscow, where he could lunch at the *Slavyansky Bazaar,* dine at the Hermitage, and wind up his day on Malaya Bronnaya Street or at the Zhivodyorka night club with the gypsies (he called this "Giving oneself a lift"). Podgorin himself drank, sometimes heavily, and was promiscuous with women, but casually, coldly, without finding any pleasure in it, and he was disgusted when other men abandoned themselves passionately in front of him. He could not understand people who felt more free at Zhivodyorka than they did at home beside decent women, and he did not care for such people; it seemed to him that they wallowed in all sorts of uncleanness which clung to them like burrs. He did not like Losev either and considered him uninteresting, an absolute lazy good-for-nothing, and he had more than once felt nauseated in his company.

Just past the woods, he was met by Sergei Sergeyich and Nadezhda.

"My dear old fellow, why have you forgotten us like this?" Sergei Sergeyich said, kissing him three times and then clasping him round the waist with both arms. "You no longer care for us, dear friend!"

He had big features, a thick nose and a skimpy fair beard; he parted his hair on the side, like a merchant, in order to look like a simple, honest Russian. When he talked, he breathed right into his listener's face, and when he was silent, he breathed heavily through his nose. His well-fed body and excessive weight hampered him, and in order to breathe more easily he was continually sticking out his chest; this gave him a haughty appearance. Nadezhda, his sister-in-law, looked quite ethereal beside him. She was slender, very fair and pale, with kind, affectionate eyes; Podgorin really did not know whether she was beautiful or not, for he had known her from her childhood and had grown used to her appearance. She was in a white dress now, open at the throat, and the effect of her white, long, bare neck was new to him and not altogether pleasing.

"My sister and I have been waiting for you since morning," she said. "Varya is staying with us, and she has been waiting too."

She took his arm and suddenly burst out laughing without any reason and gave a low, happy cry, as though all of a sudden charmed by some thought or other. The fields, thick with winter rye standing without a ripple in the still air, and the forest, lit up by the sun, were beautiful; it was as though Nadezhda had noticed this only just now, as she walked beside Podgorin.

"I've come to spend three days with you," he said. "You must forgive me, I could not get away from Moscow earlier."

"It's wrong, it's wrong of you to forget all about us," said Sergei Sergeyich in good-humored reproach. " '*Jamais de ma vie!*' " he added suddenly and snapped his fingers.

He had a mannerism, startling for the person he was speaking to, of inserting in the form of an excla-

mation some phrase or other having nothing at all to
do with the conversation, and snapping his fingers at
the same time. And he was constantly imitating somebody; if he rolled his eyes, or carelessly tossed back
his hair, or sank into pathos, this meant he had been
to the theatre the day before, or at a dinner where
there had been speech-making. Now he was walking
like a man with gout, with little mincing steps and
without bending his knees—probably he was imitating
someone now, too.

"You know, Tanya didn't believe you would come,"
said Nadezhda. "But Varya and I had a premonition; somehow I knew you would come on this very
train."

" '*Jamais de ma vie!*' " repeated Sergei Sergeyich.

The other ladies were waiting on the terrace in the
garden. Ten years ago Podgorin—he was a poor student then—had coached Nadezhda in mathematics
and history in return for his board and lodging, and
Varya, who was attending a girls' college, took Latin
lessons from him on the side. But Tanya, already a
beautiful grown-up girl by then, thought of nothing
but love, desired only love and happiness, desired it
passionately, and was waiting for the bridegroom she
dreamed of day and night. And now, when she was
over thirty, as beautiful and as striking as ever, in a
full peignoir, with plump white arms, she thought
only of her husband and her two little daughters; and
her expression suggested that, even though she might
be talking and smiling, nonetheless she was keeping
her thoughts to herself, nonetheless she was on watch
over this love and her right to this love, and was ready
at any moment to hurl herself on any enemy who
might wish to take her husband and children from
her. She loved her husband ardently, and it seemed to
her that the love was mutual; yet jealousy, and fear
for her children, tortured her ceaselessly and prevented
her from being happy.

After the noisy greetings on the terrace, everyone

except Sergei Sergeyich went into Tatyana's room. The sun's rays could not penetrate here, through the lowered blinds; it was twilight, so that all the roses in a large bouquet seemed of one color. They made Podgorin sit down in an old armchair by the window. Nadezhda sat on a low footstool at his feet. He knew that besides the soft reproaches, jests, and laughter which reminded him so much of the past, there would still be an unpleasant discussion about promissory notes and mortgages—this was unavoidable—and he reflected that it might be better to talk over business matters right now rather than to put them off; get it over with quickly and—afterward—get away into the garden, into the open air . . .

"Shouldn't we talk about business first?" he said. "What is there new at Kuzminky? Is everything prospering in the state of Denmark?"

"Things are bad with us at Kuzminky," Tatyana answered and sighed mournfully. "Oh, our affairs are in such a dreadful state, it seems they couldn't be worse," she said, pacing up and down the room in agitation. "Our estate is up for sale, the auction is set for the seventh of August, it has already been advertised all over, and buyers are arriving here, going all through the rooms, looking at everything . . . Everybody has the right now to go into my room and look around. It may be right, according to the law, but it humiliates me; it's profoundly insulting. We have nothing to pay with and no one to borrow from any longer. In a word, it's horrible, horrible! I swear to you," she went on, halting in the middle of the room, her voice trembling and her eyes filling with tears, "I swear to you by all I hold sacred, by my children's happiness, I can't live without Kuzminky! I was born here, this is my nest, and if they take it away from me I shall not survive it. I shall die of grief."

"It seems to me you're taking too gloomy a view," said Podgorin. "Everything will turn out all right.

Your husband will take a job with the government, you will settle into a new routine and start a new life."

"How can you say that!" cried Tatyana. Now she looked very beautiful and strong, and her face and her whole figure expressed most vividly her readiness to hurl herself at any moment on any enemy who might wish to take her husband, her children and her nest away from her. "What kind of new life would that be! Sergei is looking for a position, he has been promised a place as tax inspector somewhere in the district of Ufa or Perm, and I am ready to go anywhere, even to Siberia; I am prepared to live there ten, twenty years, but I must be sure that sooner or later, in spite of everything, I shall come back to Kuzminky. I can't live without Kuzminky. I can't and I don't want to. I don't want to!" she cried and stamped her foot.

"Misha, you're a lawyer," said Varya. "You're sharp, and it's up to you to advise us what to do."

There was only one truthful and rational answer, "There's nothing to be done." But Podgorin could not bring himself to say it outright, and he mumbled irresolutely, "This will have to be thought over . . . I'll think about it."

There were two men in him. It had fallen to him as a lawyer to handle some rough cases, and in the law court and with his clients he conducted himself haughtily and always expressed his opinion plainly and sharply. Among his everyday companions he affected rudeness, but in his personal, intimate life, among those close to him or with people he had known a long time, he revealed an unusual delicacy, with them he was shy and sensitive and unable to speak bluntly. A single tear, a side glance, a lie or even a clumsy gesture was enough to make his heart contract and his will power evaporate. Now Nadezhda was sitting at his feet, and her bare neck displeased him, and this disturbed him; he even wanted to go home. One day a year ago he had run into Sergei Sergeyich at a certain lady's on Bronnaya Street, and now he felt awkward in front of

Tatyana, as though he himself had been an accomplice in the betrayal. This conversation about Kuzminky presented him with a great problem. He was accustomed to having all delicate and unpleasant questions resolved by a judge or a jury or simply by some article of law; whenever a question was presented to him personally, for his own solution, he was at a loss.

"Misha, you're our friend, we all love you like one of the family," Tatyana went on, "and I will tell you quite frankly: you are our only hope. Will you for God's sake tell us what to do? Maybe we should submit an application somewhere? Maybe it's still not too late to transfer the estate to Nadya's or Varya's name? . . . What shall we do?"

"Help us, Misha, help us," said Varya, lighting a cigarette. "You were always so bright. You've lived very little, you still haven't had any experience of life, but you have a good head on your shoulders . . . You will help Tanya, I know."

"I'll have to think it over . . . Possibly I may think up something."

They went out for a stroll in the garden and afterward in the fields. Sergei Sergeyich came along too. He took Podgorin by the arm and continually pulled him on ahead, apparently intending to talk something over with him, probably the bad state of affairs. But to walk beside Sergei Sergeyich and talk to him was torture. Every now and again he kissed Podgorin—always three times—took his arm, clasped him around the waist, and breathed into his face; and it seemed as if he were covered with a sugary glue and in a minute would be stuck fast to you; the expression in his eyes, hinting that he needed something from Podgorin, that he was on the point of asking him for something, created a painful impression as though he were taking aim with a pistol.

The sun had set, it began to grow dark. Here and there along the railroad tracks lights flashed, green, red . . . Varya stopped and, as she looked at the lights, began to quote:

> Straight is the railroad: the narrow embankments,
> The milestones, bridges and rails,
> And to either side, everywhere, lie Russian bones . . .
> How many there are![1] . . .

"How does it go on? Oh, good lord, I've forgotten everything!"

> We have worn ourselves out in the heat, in the cold,
> With backs everlastingly stooped . . .

She recited in a splendid deep voice, with feeling; a lively blush lit up her face, and tears came to her eyes. Here was the old Varya, Varya the college girl, and as he listened to her, Podgorin thought of the past and remembered how he himself, when a student, knew many fine poems by heart and loved to recite them.

> His bent back he has never straightened
> To this very day: dull and silent . . .

But Varya could not remember any more . . . She fell silent and smiled weakly and listlessly, and after her recitation the green and red lights took on a mournful aspect.

"Oh, I've forgotten it!"

Podgorin, however, had suddenly remembered it, as though it had accidentally survived in his memory from his student years, and he recited softly, in a low tone:

> The people of Russia have borne enough,
> And the railroad, too, they will bear,—
> They will suffer it all—and a broad, shining path
> They will carve for themselves with their breasts . . .
> 'Tis only a pity . . .

[1] "The Railroad," a poem by Nikolai Alexeyevich Nekrasov (1821–1877).

" ' 'Tis only a pity,' " Varya interrupted him, having remembered it. " ' 'Tis only a pity neither thou nor I will live in that marvelous age!' "

And she suddenly laughed and clapped him on the shoulder.

They returned to the house and sat down to supper. Sergei Sergeyich tucked the corner of his napkin carelessly into his collar in imitation of someone or other.

"Let's have a drink," he said, pouring out vodka for himself and Podgorin. "We old students knew how to drink and how to talk and how to do our work. I drink your health, my old friend, and you shall drink the health of an old fool of an idealist and wish that he may die an idealist. Only the grave can cure a hunchback."

Tatyana looked tenderly at her husband all through supper, jealous and uneasy lest he should eat or drink something bad for him. It seemed to her that he had been spoiled by women, that he was tired—she liked this in him, but at the same time she suffered. Varya and Nadya were also tender with Sergei and looked at him anxiously, as if they were afraid he would suddenly take off and leave them. When he wished to pour himself a second drink, Varya put on a stern face and said:

"You are poisoning yourself, Sergei Sergeyich. You are a highly strung, sensitive person and it would be easy for you to become an alcoholic. Tanya, have them take the vodka away."

Sergei Sergeyich generally had great success with women. They loved his height, his build, his big features, his indolence and his misfortunes. They said that he was very goodhearted, and that was why he was a spendthrift; that he was an idealist and therefore impractical; that he was an honest, pure soul unable to adapt himself to people and circumstances, and that was why he owned nothing and could not find himself any definite work. They trusted him implicitly, worshiped him and spoiled him with their adoration, until he himself began to believe that he was an idealist, an impractical, honest, pure soul, and in every way higher and better than these women.

"Why haven't you complimented my little girls?" said Tatyana, looking lovingly at her two healthy, well-fed little daughters, who resembled two butter balls, as she set before them dishes filled with rice. "Just look at them! They say all mothers praise their children, but I assure you, I am not biased—my little girls *are* extraordinary. Especially the elder one."

Podgorin smiled at her and at the little girls, but it seemed strange to him that this young, healthy, sensible woman, such a great, complex organism, should be spending all her energy and all her strength on such a simple, small task as the organization of this nest, which was quite well enough organized as it was.

Perhaps this is the way things have to be, he thought, but it is uninteresting and unintelligent.

" 'Before he could gasp, he was in the bear's clasp,[2] ' " said Sergei Sergeyich, quoting Krilov's fable, and snapped his fingers.

They finished supper. Tatyana and Varya made Podgorin sit down on a couch in the drawing room and began talking to him about business again, in undertones.

"We must save Sergei Sergeyich," said Varya, "it is our moral duty. He has his weaknesses, he is improvident, he doesn't think of preparing for a rainy day, but it's all because he is so kind and generous. He has the soul of a child. If you gave him a million, in a month he would have nothing left. He would have given it all away."

"It's true, it's true," said Tatyana, and tears ran down her cheeks. "I have suffered a great deal for him, but I must admit he's a wonderful man."

And neither Tatyana nor Varya could refrain from

---

[2] From Krilov's well-known fable, "The Peasant and the Farmhand" (in which a man goes out to catch a bear and the bear catches him).

a little stroke of cruelty in reproaching Podgorin, "But your generation is no longer like that, Misha!"

What has this got to do with generations? thought Podgorin. Losev is only six years older than I, no more . . .

"It's not easy to live in this world," said Varya and sighed. "A man is continually threatened by some loss or other. Either they want to take your estate away from you, or one of your dear ones becomes sick and you are afraid he will die—and so it goes day after day. But what is one to do, my friends? We must submit to the will of the Almighty without complaining; we must remember that nothing in this world happens by chance, that everything has its remote purpose. You've had very little experience of life yet, Misha. You've suffered very little and you will laugh at me; go ahead and laugh, I will say it anyway—just when I was the most consumed with anxiety I have had several instances of clairvoyance, and this has caused a revolution in my soul and now I know that nothing happens by chance, that everything that happens in our lives is necessary."

This Varya, already gray, laced up in a corset, wearing a fashionable dress with short puffed sleeves, Varya twisting a cigarette in her long thin fingers, which for some reason were trembling, Varya lightly falling into mysticism, speaking so listlessly and monotonously—how different was this Varya from Varya the college girl, red-headed, gay, noisy, daring . . .

And where has it all disappeared to! thought Podgorin, listening to her with boredom.

"Sing something, Va," he said, to bring this talk about clairvoyance to an end. "You used to sing very well once."

"Oh, Misha, those days are gone."

"All right, then recite something from Nekrasov."

"I've forgotten it all. That thing came to me earlier by accident."

In spite of the corset and the short sleeves, it was plain that she was hard up and half-starving in her factory near Tula. And it was very plain that she was overworked; her hard, monotonous labor, together with her eternal interference in the affairs of others and her anxiety for her friends had tired and aged her, so that Podgorin, as he looked at her faded, sorrowful face, thought that actually it was not Kuzminky nor Sergei Sergeyich, whose cause she was pleading, who should be helped, but she herself.

It seemed that higher education and the fact that she had become a physician had not affected her as a woman. Just like Tatyana she loved weddings, births, christenings and long talks about children; she loved scary novels with happy endings, and read the papers only for the fires, floods and ceremonial festivals; she badly wanted Podgorin to propose to Nadezhda, and would have burst into tears of joy if this had come about.

He did not know whether it happened by chance or whether Varya had arranged it, but he found himself alone with Nadezhda. Yet the very suspicion that they were watching him and wanted something from him embarrassed and disturbed him, and he felt, beside Nadezhda, as though they had been put in one cage together.

"Let's go into the garden," she said.

They went into the garden; he—reluctantly, with a feeling of annoyance, not knowing what to talk to her about, and she—happy and proud to be near him, obviously pleased that he was going to stay another three days here, and filled, probably, with sweet dreams and hopes. He did not know whether or not she loved him, but he did know that she had grown used to him and attached to him a long time ago and still saw him as her teacher, and that her heart was filled now with the same emotions that had moved her sister Tatyana years ago; that is, she now thought of nothing but love, of being married very soon and having a hus-

band, children and a home of her own. She had re-
tained to this day that feeling of close friendship which
is sometimes so strong in children, and it was very
likely that she only respected Podgorin and loved him
as a friend, having fallen in love not with him, but with
these very dreams of a husband and children.

"It's beginning to get dark," he said.

"Yes. The moon rises late now."

They were walking all the time along a single path-
way near the house. Podgorin did not wish to go into
the depths of the garden; it was so dark there he would
have to take Nadezhda by the arm, be very close to
her. Shadows were moving on the terrace, and it
seemed to him that Tatyana and Varya were watching
him.

"I must ask your advice," said Nadezhda, coming to
a halt. "If Kuzminky is sold, then Sergei Sergeyich
will go into government service and our life will be
completely changed. I shan't go with my sister; we
shall part, because I don't want to be a burden to her
family. I shall have to work. I'll get a job somewhere
in Moscow—earn a salary and help my sister and her
husband. You will help me with your advice, won't
you?"

Completely unaccustomed to work, she was now inspired by the idea of an independent life; she was
making plans for the future—it was written in her
face—and this life, when she would be working and
helping others, seemed wonderful and poetic to her.
He saw her pale face and dark eyebrows very close to
him and remembered what an intelligent, quick-witted
student she had been, how full of promise, and how
pleasant it had been to give her lessons. Here, probably,
was no ordinary young woman who wished for a husband, but an intelligent, noble girl, extraordinarily kind,
with a gentle, soft heart, out of whom, as from wax,
one could mold anything one wished, and who would
grow into a superb woman, once given the right sur-
roundings.

Really, why shouldn't I marry her? thought Podgorin, but immediately, for some reason, he was frightened by the thought and went back to the house.

Tatyana was sitting at the grand piano in the drawing room, and her playing vividly recalled the past, when in this very drawing room they would play, sing and dance until the small hours, with the windows flung wide, and the birds in the garden and by the river would be singing too. Podgorin cheered up, began to fool around, danced with Nadezhda and Varya and afterward sang. A corn on his foot bothered him and he asked permission to put on Sergei Sergeyich's slippers; strange to say, in the slippers he began to feel really one of the family—Just like a brother-in-law, flashed into his mind—and he became still happier. As they looked at him they all revived and cheered up, as though they had grown younger. Their faces began to glow with hope: Kuzminky would be saved! Really it was so simple; someone had only to think up something, to dip into the law books or to marry off Nadya to Podgorin . . . And obviously things were already moving forward. Nadya, rosy and happy, her eyes full of tears in anticipation of something quite out of the ordinary, whirled in the dance, her white dress billowing out and revealing her lovely slender legs in flesh-colored stockings . . . Varya, very pleased, took Podgorin by the arm and said to him in a low voice with a meaningful expression:

"Misha, don't run away from your happiness. Take hold of it when it puts itself in your hands, for afterward, even though you may chase after it, it will be too late—you will not catch up with it."

Podgorin felt like making promises and encouraging hopes, and by now he even believed, himself, that Kuzminky could be saved and that it was a simple thing to do.

" 'And you will be-e-e-e-e the queen of the wo-o-o-orld,[3] ' " he began to sing, adopting a pose, and then

[3] "The Demon," Part II, by Mikhail Yurievich Lermontov (1814–1841).

all at once he remembered that nothing could be done for these people, absolutely nothing, and he grew quiet like a guilty person.

Afterward he sat silently in a corner, with his feet, in the borrowed slippers, crossed under him.

As they looked at him the rest of them understood, too, that nothing could be done, and they became very quiet. They closed the piano. Everyone remarked that it was already late, that it was time to go to bed, and Tatyana put out the big lamp in the drawing room.

A bed had been prepared for Podgorin in the same wing where he had lived long ago. Sergei Sergeyich went along to lead the way, holding the candle high above his head, although by now the moon was coming up and it was light. They walked along the avenue between the lilac bushes, and the gravel rustled under their feet.

" 'Before he could gasp, he was in the bear's clasp,' " said Sergei Sergeyich.

It seemed to Podgorin that he had heard this phrase a thousand times by now. He was sick of it! When they reached the wing, Sergei Sergeyich pulled out of his roomy jacket a bottle and two glasses and set them on the table.

"It's cognac," he said. "Five star. It's impossible to take a drink with Varya in the house, she starts off at once about alcoholism; but here we're free. It's splendid cognac."

They sat down. The cognac indeed turned out to be excellent.

"Let's drink hearty today," went on Sergei Sergeyich, chewing on slices of lemon between drinks. "I'm the old student type, I like to have fun once in a while. One needs it!"

But there was the same look in his eyes, as if he needed something from Podgorin and was on the point of asking him for it.

"Let's drink up, old fellow," he went on with a sigh. "Things have turned out so badly I have to take it.

For us old eccentrics the end has come, the roof has fallen in. Idealism is not in vogue now. The ruble is king now, and if you don't want to be pushed out of the way, you must fling yourself down before the ruble and grovel. I can't do it. It's sickening!"

"When is the sale arranged for?" asked Podgorin, to change the subject.

"The seventh of August. But I'm not counting on saving Kuzminky, my dear. There's a tremendous pile of arrears and the estate doesn't bring in any income, only losses every year. It's not worth it . . . Tanya is sorry, of course, it's her ancestral home, but I admit I am even glad in a way. I'm not cut out for village life at all. My sphere is the great, noisy city; my element, the fight!"

He went on talking, but still without saying what he wanted, and he watched Podgorin closely as though only waiting for an opportune moment. And suddenly Podgorin saw his eyes very near, felt his breath on his face . . .

"Save me, my dear!" Sergei Sergeyich muttered, breathing heavily. "Give me two hundred rubles! I beg of you!"

Podgorin felt like saying that he was pressed for money himself, and he reflected that it would be better to give those two hundred rubles to some poor man or even to lose it at cards; but he was terribly embarrassed and, feeling as though he were in a trap in this tiny room with its single candle, and wanting to rid himself quickly of that breathing, of those soft hands that clasped him round the waist and already seemed to be sticking to him, he began quickly looking in his pockets for his notebook, where his money was.

"Here . . ." he muttered, taking out a hundred rubles. "You will get the rest later. I have no more on me. You see, I can't say no," he added with irritation, beginning to get angry. "I have an impossible character, like an old woman's. Only do pay me back later, please. I'm hard up myself."

"Thank you. *Thank* you, old man!"

"And for God's sake stop fancying yourself as an idealist. It you're an idealist, I'm a turkey. You're just an irresponsible loafer and nothing else."

Sergei Sergeyich sighed deeply and sat down on the sofa.

"My dear, you are angry with me," he said, "but if you only knew how wretched I am! I'm going through a horrible time just now. I swear, my dear, it's not myself I'm sorry for, no! I'm sorry for my wife and children. If it weren't for my children and my wife, I would have done away with myself long ago."

And suddenly his head and shoulders began to shake, and he burst into sobs.

"That would be the last straw," said Podgorin, walking agitatedly up and down the room and feeling intensely annoyed. "What on earth can one do with a man who has caused a great deal of harm and then sobs about it? Your tears disarm me, I haven't the heart to say anything to you. You are sobbing . . . that means you must be in the right."

"*I* have caused a great deal of harm?" asked Sergei Sergeyich, standing up and looking at Podgorin in astonishment. "Dear man, how can you say that? *I* have caused a lot of harm? Oh, how little you know me! How little you understand me!"

"Fine, maybe I don't understand you. Only, please, don't sob. It's disgusting."

"Oh, how little you know me!" repeated Losev, with perfect sincerity. "How little you know me!"

"Take a look at yourself in the glass," went on Podgorin. "You're no longer a young man, you will soon be old. It's time to take stock of yourself, to realize something, at least, of who you are and what you are. Your whole life spent doing nothing, your whole life given over to this idle, childish chattering, clowning, putting on airs—isn't your own head spinning, aren't you fed up with living this way, really? I'm sick of you! Bored to death with you!"

After he had said this Podgorin left the wing and slammed the door. For almost the first time in his life he had been candid and said what he wanted to.

A few moments later he was already sorry that he had been so harsh. What was the good of speaking seriously or arguing with a man who continually lied, ate too much, drank too much, wasted other people's money and at the same time was convinced that he was an idealist and a sufferer? It all sprang from foolishness or from old bad habits which were strongly entrenched in the organism, like a disease, and by now incurable. In any case, indignation and harsh reproaches were no use here, and it would be better to laugh at him; one good sneer would do far more than a dozen sermons!

It would be simpler not to pay the matter any attention at all, Podgorin thought, but the main thing is, not to give him any money.

But a moment later he was no longer thinking of Sergei Sergeyich or his hundred rubles. It was a night made for dreaming, quiet and very bright. When Podgorin looked up at the sky on moonlight nights, it seemed to him that only he and the moon were awake, everything else was asleep or drowsing; and he stopped thinking about people and money, and little by little his spirit grew quiet and tranquil; he felt himself all alone in the world, and in the silence of the night the sound of his own footsteps seemed to him full of sadness.

The garden was enclosed by a white stone wall. On the side leading into the open country, in the right-hand corner, stood a watch tower. The lower part of it was stone but the top was wooden, with a little platform, a conical roof and a tall steeple on which a weathercock stood out darkly. Downstairs were two doors, through which one could pass from the garden into the fields; a stairway that squeaked under one's feet led up to the platform from below. Under the stairs was a pile of old broken-down armchairs, and the light of the moon entering now through the doorway was shining on these chairs, and with their crooked broken legs sticking up in the air they seemed to have come to life in the night and to be lying in wait for someone in the stillness.

Podgorin climbed the stairs to the platform and sat down. Immediately beyond the wall was the boundary ditch with a bank, and beyond that lay the open fields, stretching far and wide, flooded with moonlight. Podgorin knew that the forest lay directly before him, three versts from the estate, and now it seemed to him he could see a dark line in the distance. Quail and corncrakes were crying, and now and again from the edge of the forest came the call of a cuckoo that was also awake.

A dog began barking. Someone was coming across the garden, drawing near the tower.

"Zhuk!" a woman's voice called softly. "Zhuk, come back!"

Below, Podgorin could hear the footsteps of someone entering the tower, and a moment later a black dog, an old friend of Podgorin's, appeared on the bank. It stopped, looked up at the place where Podgorin was sitting and began wagging its tail in a friendly way. A few moments later a white figure arose out of the black ditch like a shadow and also stopped on the bank. It was Nadezhda.

"What do you see there?" she asked the dog, and began looking intently upward.

She did not see Podgorin but probably she sensed his nearness for she was smiling, and her pale face, illumined by the moon, looked happy. The black shadow of the tower, stretching along the ground far into the fields, the motionless white figure with the blissful smile on its pale face, the black dog, their two shadows—all of it together was like a dream . . .

"There is someone there," Nadezhda murmured softly.

She stood there waiting for him to come down or to call her up to him and at last declare himself, so that they could both be happy on this quiet, glorious night. White, wan, slender and very beautiful in the moonlight, she was expecting tenderness; her constant dreams of happiness and love had exhausted her, and by now it was beyond her power to conceal her feelings; her whole figure, the brilliance of her eyes and her fixed happy smile betrayed her secret thoughts. As for him, he felt uncomfortable, he shrank into himself and was quiet, and did not know whether to speak up and pass it all off as a joke, as usual, or to keep silent; he was annoyed with himself and could only think that here in this country estate, on a moonlight night, beside a beautiful girl in love and dreaming, he was as unmoved as on his visits to Malaya Bronnaya Street, because evidently all this poetry had lost its meaning for him just as the coarse prose had. And there was no longer any meaning for him either in moonlight meetings, or in slim-waisted white figures, or in mysterious shadows, or in watchtowers and country estates, or in such "types" as Sergei Sergeyich, or in the kind of people such as he, Podgorin, had himself become, with his cold boredom, his eternal discontent, his inability to adjust to real life and to take what it offered him, and his painful, aching hunger for what did not and could not exist on earth. And as he sat there in the tower, he felt he would have much preferred to see a display of fireworks, or some procession or other under the moonlight, or hear Varya again reciting "The Railroad"; or he would have preferred another woman to stand there on the bank, where Nadezhda was standing now, and speak about something interesting and new, having nothing to do with love or happiness. Yet at the same time if she *were* to speak of love, it would be to call for a new form of life, lofty and intelligent, on the eve of which we are perhaps already living, and of which we have a presentiment now and again.

"There is no one there," said Nadezhda.

And after waiting another minute, she walked away in the direction of the forest, in silence, her head drooping. The dog ran on in front of her. Podgorin could see the little patch of white for a long time afterward.

Strange, how it all came out! he kept thinking to himself as he made his way back to his room in the wing.

He could not imagine what he could say to Sergei Sergeyich or to Tatyana, or how he was to behave toward Nadezhda tomorrow, and the day after tomorrow too—and he began to suffer the embarrassment, fear and boredom in advance. How was he to fill in those long three days he had promised to spend here? He remembered the conversation about clairvoyance and Sergei Sergeyich's phrase: "Before he could gasp, he was in the bear's clasp"; he remembered that tomorrow, to please Tatyana, he would have to smile at her well-fed, plump little girls—and he decided to leave.

At half-past six Sergei Sergeyich appeared on the terrace of the big house in a Bokharan dressing gown and a fez with a tassel. Podgorin, without wasting a minute, walked over to him and began to say goodbye.

"I have to be in Moscow at ten o'clock," he said, not meeting the other's eyes. "I had completely forgotten they will be expecting me at the notary's office. You must please excuse me. When your family gets up, please give them my apologies, I'm terribly sorry . . ."

He did not hear what Sergei Sergeyich said to him and hurried away, looking back over his shoulder at the windows of the big house all the time, afraid lest the ladies should wake up and detain him. He was ashamed of his nervousness. He felt that he was seeing Kuzminky for the last time, and that he would never come back here again; and as he was leaving he glanced back several times at the wing where he had once passed so many happy days, but his heart was cold; he felt no sorrow.

At home the first thing he noticed was the note he had read yesterday, lying on the desk. "My dear Misha," he read, "You have utterly forgotten us; do come and pay us a visit right away . . ."

And for no reason he recalled how Nadezhda had whirled in the dance, and how her dress had billowed out, revealing her legs in flesh-colored stockings . . .

Ten minutes later he was already sitting at his desk, working, and no longer thinking about Kuzminky at all.

From STANISLAVSKI'S LEGACY

Edited and translated by Elizabeth Reynolds Hapgood

Messages about *The Cherry Orchard* from Stanislavski to Chekhov

Telegram: October 20, 1903

I have just read the play. Deeply moved, scarcely control myself. Am in unheard-of state of enthusiasm. Consider the play the finest of all the things you have written. Cordial congratulations to the genius author. I feel, I treasure every word. Thank you for the great pleasure already received and also in store.

Letter: same date

Dear Anton Pavlovich:

According to me, your *Cherry Orchard* is your best play. I have fallen in love with it even more deeply than with our dear *Seagull*. It is not a comedy, not a farce, as you wrote—it is a tragedy, no matter if you do indicate a way out into a better world in the last act. It makes a tremendous impression, and this by means of halftones, tender watercolor tints. There is a poetic and lyric quality to it, very theatrical; all the parts, including that of the vagrant, are brilliant. If I were to choose one of the parts to suit my taste, I would be in a quandary, for every one of them is most alluring. I fear this is all too subtle for the public. It will take time for it to understand the shadings.

Alas, how many stupidities we will have to hear about this play! Nevertheless, it will have a tremendous success because as a play it holds you. It is so completely a whole, one cannot delete a single word from it. It may be that I am prejudiced, yet I cannot find any defect in this play. Oh, yes, there is one: it requires too great, too subtle actors to bring out all its charms. We shall not be able to do that. When we had our first reading together, I was worried by one thing: I was instantly carried away and my feelings caught up by the play. This was not the case with *The Seagull* or *The Three Sisters.* I am accustomed to a rather vague impression from a first reading of your plays. That is why I was afraid that, when I read it for the second time, it would not capture me again. Nothing of the sort happened. I wept like a woman, I tried to control myself, but could not. I can hear you say: "But please, this is a farce. . . ." No, for the ordinary person this is a tragedy. I sense an attitude of a very special kind of tenderness and affection toward this play. I scarcely heard a word of criticism, yet you know how actors love to be critical. Apparently this time they were all instantly won by it. If someone by chance does utter a word of criticism, I merely smile and do not bother to argue. I am only sorry for the critic. Someone said: the fourth is the best act, and the second is least successful. I have only to go over the second act, scene by scene, and that critic is demolished. The fourth act is good just because the second act is magnificent, and vice versa. I proclaim this play *hors concours,* and not subject to criticism. Anyone who does not see that is a fool. That is my sincere conviction. I shall act in it with delight. If I could do so, I should love to play all the parts, including that of dear Charlotte. Thank you, dear Anton Pavlovich, for the immense pleasure you have already given and for that which is yet to come. How I wish I could give up everything else, shake off the yoke of playing Brutus, and work on nothing but *The Cherry Orchard* all day.

This horrible Brutus weighs on me and draws all the juice out of me. I hate him more than ever after (reading) the sweet *Cherry Orchard.*

My warm regards to you, and I beg you not to take me for a neurotic lady admirer.

Your affectionate and devoted,
C. Alexeyev [Stanislavski]

Letter: November 2, 1903

I think I have just found the set for the first act. It is a very difficult set. The windows must be close enough to the front of the stage so that the cherry orchard will be seen from the entire auditorium; there are three doors; one would wish to show a bit of Anya's room, bright and virginal. The room is a passageway, but one must be made to feel that here (in the nursery) it is cozy, warm, and light; the room has fallen into disuse, there is a slight sense of vacancy about it. Moreover the set must be comfortable and contain a number of planned acting areas. I think we are now able to encompass all this. Do you remember that last year Simov showed you a model which was made for the Turgenev play, *Where the Thread Is Thin, It Breaks?* At the time we decided, with your approval, to save the set for the last act of your play. I have been looking at the model now and find that, with a few alterations, it is very suitable (for the fourth act). If you recall the model, have you any objections? As I write, the third act of *Uncle Vanya* is beginning. There is an enthusiastic response to it, it's the eighty-ninth performance, and we took in 1400 rubles today despite the fact that last night we played *The Three Sisters.* So you have earned one hundred and forty rubles today. That's not important. But do you know what is important? It's that this year as never before the audience is really understanding you, they listen in absolute silence. Not a cough in the house despite the bad weather.

Letter: November 19, 1903

... I have been busy, working on the second act and finally have it in shape. I think it has come out charmingly. Let's hope the scenery will be successful. The little chapel, the ravine, the neglected cemetery in the middle of an oasis of trees in the open steppes. The left side and the centre will not have any wings. You will see only the far horizon. This will be produced by a single semicircular backdrop with attachments to deepen the perspective. In the distance you see the flash of a stream and the manor house on a slight rise, telegraph poles, and a railroad bridge. Do let us have a train go by with a puff of smoke in one of the pauses. That might turn out very well. Before sundown there will be a brief glimpse of the town, and toward the end of the act, a fog: it will be particularly thick above the ditch downstage. The frogs and corncrakes will strike up at the very end of the act. To the left in the foreground, a mown field and a small mound of hay, on which the scene is played by the group out walking. This is for the actors, it will help them get into the spirit of their parts. The general tone of the set is like that of a Levitan painting. The landscape is that of the province of Orel not of lower Kursk.

The work is now being carried on as follows: Nemirovich-Danchenko rehearsed the first act yesterday, and today I wrote (the plan for) the following acts. I haven't rehearsed my own part yet. I am still undecided about the set for acts three and four. The model is made and came out well, it is full of mood, and besides it is laid out so that all parts of it are visible to all in the auditorium. Down front there is something like shrubbery. Farther upstage are the stairs and billiard room. The windows are painted on the walls. This set is more convenient for the ball. Still a small voice keeps whispering in my ear that if we have one set, which we change in the fourth act, it would be easier and cozier to play in. The weather, alas, is murderous. Everything is melting again and it rains frequently.

Yours,
C. Alexeyev

Telegram from St. Petersburg: April 2, 1904

Success of *Cherry Orchard* very great, incomparably greater than in Moscow. After third act there were insistent calls for author. The connoisseurs are rapturous over play. Newspapers not very understanding. Company in high spirits. I am triumphant. Congratulations.

                                                              Alexeyev

From MY LIFE IN ART

by Konstantin Stanislavski

"THE CHERRY ORCHARD"

Is it necessary to describe the production of "The Cherry Orchard"? We have played it so often in Europe and America. But I will say some things about it, not for the sake of following the line of the evolution of the Moscow Art Theatre in it, but in order to tell of the last year in the life of Chekhov and of his death which had a tremendous importance in the life of our Theatre.

The production of "The Cherry Orchard" was accomplished with great hardships. The play is delicate, it has all the tenderness of a flower. Break its stem and the flower dries, its odor vanishes. The play and the rôles live only when the stage director and the artist dig deep enough to reach the secret treasure house of the human spirit in which is hidden the chief nerve of the play. In my great desire to help the actors I tried to create a mood around them, in the hope that it would grip them and call forth creative vision. In those days our inner technique and our ability of reacting on another's creative soul were very primitive. I took all the bypaths I could think of. I invented all sorts of *mises en scène,* the singing of birds, the barking of dogs, and in this enthusiasm for sounds on the stage I went so far that I caused a protest on the part of Chekhov, who loved sounds on the stage himself. The form in which he expressed his disagreement with me was very interesting.

" 'What fine quiet,' the chief person of my play will say," he said to some one so that I could hear him. " 'How wonderful! We hear no birds, no dogs, no cuckoos, no owls, no clocks, no sleigh bells, no crickets.' "

That stone was intended for my garden.

Nemirovich-Danchenko and I did not think that the production would be ripe at its first performance. And meanwhile, until the play was produced, it risked becoming boresome. The success of the play was necessary at all costs, for the health of Anton Pavlovich was in a precarious condition. So we decided to take advantage of the jubilee of Chekhov's literary activity and to stage the first night of the play on that day. Our reckoning was simple. If the actors were not able to put the play over, its failure of great success could be blamed on the unusual conditions of the jubilee evening which would not fail to draw the attention of the spectators away from the actors to the author. But the appointed date was very near and the play was not yet ready. Besides, I had to think of a present for Anton Pavlovich. This was a hard question to settle. I visited all the antiquaries in Moscow, hoping to find something, but outside of some very fine embroidered cloth I found nothing. As there was nothing better, we decorated the jubilee wreath with this cloth. "At least," I thought, "we will present him with something of artistic value."

But Anton Pavlovich never forgot this gift.

"Listen, this is a wonderful thing, it must be kept in a museum," he upbraided me after the jubilee.

"Tell me, Anton Pavlovich, what should we have given you?" I asked in my confusion.

"A rat trap," he answered seriously, after thinking for some time. "Listen, mice must be destroyed." Here he began laughing himself. "Korovin sent me a beautiful present, a beautiful one!"

"What was it?" I became interested.

"Fishing poles."

None of the other presents he received pleased Chekhov, and some of them angered him with their banality.

"Listen, one shouldn't give a writer a silver pen and an ancient inkwell."

"Well, what should one give?"

"A piece of rubber pipe. Listen, I am a doctor. Or socks. My wife doesn't attend to me as she should. She is an actress. And I walk around in torn socks. 'Listen, little soul,' I say to her, 'the big toe of my right foot is coming out.' 'Wear it on your left foot,' she answers. It can't go on that way—"

And he rolled with happy laughter.

But at the jubilee he was far from happy. It seemed that he foresaw his own end. After the third act he stood deathly pale and thin on the right side of the stage and could not control his coughing while gifts were showered on him and speeches in his honor were being made. Our hearts grew small in us. Some one in the audience cried loudly that he should sit down. But he drew his brows together and stood throughout the duration of the jubilee, over which he laughed so innocently in his works. Even on that evening he could not control his smile. One of the best-known professors in Russia began his speech almost with the same words with which Gaiev greeted the old clothespress in the first act of "The Cherry Orchard."

"Dear and much respected (instead of saying clothespress, the professor used Chekhov's name)—I greet you—"

Anton Pavlovich looked sideways at me (I had played Gaiev) and a villainous smile passed over his lips.

The triumph was a really triumphant occasion, but it smelled of a funeral. Our souls were heavy within us.

The performance itself enjoyed but a mediocre success and we blamed ourselves for not having portrayed much that was in the play.

Chekhov died without ever seeing the real success of his last flowerlike play.

FURTHER NOTES ON "THE CHERRY ORCHARD"

by Konstantin Stanislavski

Translated by
Elizabeth Reynolds Hapgood

I was fortunate enough to be able to watch from the side lines the process by which Chekhov created this play, *The Cherry Orchard*. Once, while talking with Chekhov, our actor A. P. Artem acted out for him how to put a worm on a fishhook, how to throw out a line with a sinker or one with a float. These and other similar scenes were played by our inimitable Artem with great talent, and Chekhov sincerely regretted that a large theatre audience could not have seen them. Not long after this, Chekhov was present when another actor from our theatre was bathing in a river. "Listen," he thereupon announced, "Artem must fish in a play I will write while N. is bathing nearby. He will be splashing about and yelling so loudly that Artem will get annoyed for fear the fish will be frightened away."

Chekhov visualized them both on the stage—the one fishing near a swimming hole, the other splashing around in it, offstage. A few days later Chekhov solemnly announced to us that the bather had had his arm amputated, yet despite this he was crazy about playing billiards with his remaining arm. The fisherman had become an old retainer who had saved up a bit of money.

Still later Chekhov's imagination conceived of a window in an old manor house through which branches of trees came into the room. There they broke into snowy white blossoms. Then Chekhov imagined a lady as settled in the house.

"But you haven't any actress for this part," he announced. "Listen! It calls for a very special kind of an old lady. She keeps running to the old retainer to borrow money from him. . . ."

Beside the old lady there now appeared a man, an uncle perhaps, or a brother—he was the one-armed gentleman so crazy about playing billiards. He is a big baby who cannot exist without a manservant to wait on him. It so happened that once his man went away without having laid out his master's trousers, and for that reason the gentleman had to stay in bed all day. . . .

We know now how much of this was finally preserved in the play and how much disappeared without a trace, or left only a faint trace.

In the summer of 1902, when Chekhov was getting ready to write *The Cherry Orchard,* he was living with his wife, Olga Knipper-Chekhova, an actress from our theatre, in a cottage on my mother's estate, Lyubimovka. Nearby, in the household of neighbors, there was an English governess, a thin little creature with two long braids, who dressed in man's clothing. Because of this combination of factors it was difficult to discern her sex, where she came from, and her age. She treated Chekhov with great familiarity and that pleased him very much. When they met every day, they exchanged the greatest lot of nonsense. For instance, one time Chekhov assured the Englishwoman that when he was young, he was a Turk, that he had a harem, that he would shortly return to his native land to become a Pasha, and then he would send for her. Out of gratitude, as it were, this acrobatically agile Englishwoman leaped up onto Chekhov's shoulders, settled herself, and from there greeted all passersby on Chekhov's behalf, that is to say, she took off his hat to them, bowed and spoke to them like a comic clown in broken Russian. As she did this, she made Chekhov bow to them.

Anyone who has seen *The Cherry Orchard* will recognize the prototype of Charlotta in this original little person.

When I read the play, I immediately grasped this and I expressed my enthusiasm to Chekhov. How excited he was! He kept emphasizing to me that Charlotta must absolutely be a German, absolutely must be thin and tall—a woman like our actress Muratova, who did not in any way resemble the Englishwoman from whom the portrait had been drawn.

The part of Epikhodov was the synthesis of many images. The fundamental features were taken from a manservant who lived on the estate and worked for Chekhov. Chekhov often chatted with him, trying to convince him that he should get an education, that it was necessary to read and be educated. To qualify, this prototype of Epikhodov began by buying a red necktie and deciding to learn French. I cannot tell by what paths Chekhov traveled from the old retainer image to that of the stoutish, not very young Epikhodov who was in the first version of the play.[1]

But we did not have in our company an appropriate actor for such a figure. Also it was impossible not to use the gifted Moskvin in any play by Chekhov who admired him so. Yet at that time Moskvin was young and slender. The role was given to him, and this young actor molded it to his own gifts and also used some of it as an improvisation at one of our Cabbage Parties. . . . We were afraid Chekhov would be annoyed at his taking this liberty, but he roared with laughter and after the Cabbage Party said to Moskvin:

[1] In his *Recollections of Chekhov,* Stanislavsky wrote that there was another prototype of Epikhodov, who was a magician in the recreation park known as The Hermitage. He was a tall, stout fellow in a dress coat. He looked a bit drowsy but acted very successfully and with great comic skill the character of a "Failure," while doing his juggling tricks, and it was to him that the two and twenty accidents happened. This magician was an excellent actor and unfailingly aroused the keen enthusiasm of Chekhov.

"That's the very kind of a man I was writing about. Listen, it's marvelous!"

I recall that Chekhov fleshed out the part along the lines laid down by Moskvin.

The role of Trofimov, the student was also drawn from someone living in Lyubimovka when Chekhov was there.

From MY LIFE IN THE
RUSSIAN THEATRE

by *Vladimir Nemirovich-Danchenko*

He was having a tremendous success at this time.
This gave him a new charm; he was being read more
and more, and as his readers became absorbed in him
they fell in love with him. He might have refrained from
writing another ten years, yet his fame would have
grown. He was wholly occupied with the play. He had
conceived it during the previous summer, while visiting
Alekseiev in Liubimovka, in that same Liubimovka
where Stanislavsky and I had had our first conversation.
Chekhov was thinking of "The Cherry Orchard." Apart
from that, he dedicated a good portion of his time to his
favourite diversion—fishing.

Not a single play, not a single story, did he write so
slowly as "The Cherry Orchard." The subject of this
play actually seemed to him to be a vaudeville: "I
wanted to write a vaudeville piece, but it was cold. It
was so cold in the rooms that I was forced to pace back
and forth in order to keep warm." At first he saw the
play not in four acts, but in three. At the same time
he did not think we had an actress for the leading rôle.

If I write anything that resembles a play it will be a
vaudeville piece.

I manage to write four lines a day, and these with almost unendurable torments.

The weather is terrible, a roaring blizzard blows, the trees are bending. I am fairly well. I am writing. Slowly perhaps, but nevertheless writing.

I don't seem able to get warm. I tried writing in the bedroom, but nothing has come of it: my back is hot from the stove, but my chest and my arms are cold. In this exile I feel as though my character has become spoiled, and all of me, for that matter.

Ah, my darling, I say it sincerely: what a pleasure it would give me now if I could give up being a writer!

And he simply had to write, because we in Moscow insisted that at all costs we must have his play.

Yalta was a fine, enchanting little town. You could not find such a gem either in the French or the Italian Riviera, but it was remote from Moscow, remote from all those persons who were close to his soul, remote from the metropolitan din and from the metropolitan interests, to which he had gotten so used. Always cheerful, he did not feel himself to be in his element here. He had never been a person of the study. He always wanted to have people about him. Here, with one or two possible exceptions, there lived perhaps some nice enough persons, but he did not find them interesting, and they came to him, as the saying goes, "to let off steam."

In one letter he wrote me: "The tedium here is terrible. I somehow manage to forget myself by day in my work, but with evening despair comes. And when you are already playing the second act I am already in bed, and I rise while it is still dark. Imagine to yourself: it is dark, the wind howls and the rain beats against the window."

Yes, imagine to yourself: during the hour when, in his imagination, Moscow is all ablaze with evening lights, when in his favourite theatre the second act is being played, perhaps even the second act of his "The Three Sisters", at that point where the staid provincial Prozorov says: "How pleasant it would be to sit at this moment in Testov's tavern!" When the public, taking advantage of the simplest blessings of the metropolis, laments the lot of those forced to suffer in the sad, tedious backwoods, precisely then does the author who evoked these tears experience despair, as one undergoing imprisonment. And when all those whom the author speaks of have gone to sleep, he is already up; and here the wind howls, the rain beats against the window and it is still dark.

As it happens, I am writing this chapter at Yalta. I have just come from the house, which is now the Chekhov Museum. Thanks to the heroic efforts of Anton Pavlovitch's sister, the house has successfully survived the ravages of civil war. It is she, Marya Pavlovna herself, who maintains the Museum in model order. Hundreds of tourists from all the ends of the Union, young creators of a new life, daily fill it and with avid interest glance into every corner, at every portrait. The house is all white, with a white roof; it is a very good-looking house. During the thirty years following the death of the poet the garden has become astonishingly luxuriant; the trees which Chekhov himself planted have grown quite immense. His study has been left untouched. If it were not for the glass show-case on the mantel above the table, I could easily have imagined myself as speaking with Anton Pavlovitch there but a little while before. Even the calendar on his table, as it was on the last day, did not have the date torn from it. There was the familiar fireplace, upon whose stone was painted the landscape by his friend, the famous Levitan. Upon this fireplace there once used to lie the tiny paper funnels prepared each day for his spittle, which he used to throw into the flames. The immense window looked out on the garden, and from this window you glimpsed the distant sea. When Chekhov died, his sister planted a cypress before the window. Now it is tall, graceful, mighty; it is a handsome tree, and seems to guard the memory of the master, who once sat before the window and yearned.

Someone has said: "That past is nearer to eterni-ty. . . ."

Finally, on October 12: "And so at last my patience and yours triumph. The play is finished, conclusively finished, and to-morrow evening, or at the latest on the morning of the 14th, it will be sent to you to Moscow. If any changes are necessary I cannot imagine them to be of any consequence. The worst thing about the play is that it was not written at a single sitting, but during a long, long period, so that it must give the feeling of being drawn out; well, we shall see."

Afterwards he made a few changes in this swan-song, a song with the most delicate writing. The images of "The Cherry Orchard" are realistic, simple, and clear, and at the same time moulded in such a deep crystallized essence that they resemble symbols. And the entire play is so simple, so wholly real, but to such a point purified of everything superfluous and enveloped in such a lyrical quality, that it seems to me to be a symbolic poem.

After a hard struggle with his wife and the doctors, deceiving himself, imposing his own position as a doctor, Chekhov decided that it was perfectly allowable for him to come to Moscow in the winter, that for tuberculosis rain and snow were bad, and that the severe Moscow frosts did not matter. He wrote his wife:

My darling directress, sternest of wives. I promise to eat nothing but lentils; at the entrance of Nemirovitch and Vishnevsky I will rise in respect; only let me come. Really, it's revolting to live at Yalta, and I must run from the Yalta water and the magnificent Yalta air. It's about time you cultured people understood that in Yalta I always feel incomparably worse than in Moscow. If you only knew how sadly the rain beats upon the roof, and how strongly I desire to look upon my wife. And have I a wife? Where is she?

At the beginning of December (Old Style) he arrived in Moscow, during the very thick of rehearsals. He intensely desired to take a leading part in them, to be present at all their experiments, to see himself in the densest atmosphere of the theatre. He began by deriving great pleasure from this, but very soon, after four or five rehearsals, he saw that it was not so attractive for an author: at every step on the stage they irritated him, and he succeeded only in hindering the *regisseurs* and the actors. He stopped coming.

On the other hand, he felt very happy at home. His wife was near him, and the people who came were the sort he liked, the sort that brought something instead of taking from him. He was surrounded by them the whole time.

And again he was nervous over his play, and again he doubted its success. "Buy my play for 3,000 rubles for all time," he suggested to me, without jesting.

"I'll give you," I replied, "ten thousand for a single season, and that for the Art Theatre alone." He rejected the proposal and, as always, merely shook his head.

"The Cherry Orchard" became the brightest, most expressive symbol of the Art Theatre.

The first performance took place on his name-day. This was quite accidental, without any divination or presentiment. Chekhov did not come to the theatre, but asked that any message be delivered to him over the telephone. But Moscow had the foreboding that this would be the last time in which it could see its beloved writer. They, in the city, knew that his malady of the lungs and intestines was becoming increasingly serious. All of literary and theatrical Moscow, as well as representatives of social institutions, were gathered in the theatre to do honour to the beloved writer. We telephoned to Chekhov asking him to come. At first he would not be persuaded, but when some of us went to his house and talked to him he was prevailed upon to change his mind. The tribute paid him was profoundly touching and profoundly sincere. I addressed him, speaking for the theatre:

"Our theatre is in such a degree indebted to your genius, your tender heart, your pure soul, that you can justly say: 'This is my theatre, the theatre of Chekhov.' "

In the middle of February he returned to his house in Yalta and from there, right through to the summer, his letters were no longer so tired as those of the preceding two winters; they were cheerful, gay, notwithstanding the fact that he was not quite satisfied with some of the actors in "The Cherry Orchard." It was as if a mountain had rolled from his shoulders, as if suddenly he felt he had a right to live, even as the simplest inhabitant—without any kind of literary or theatrical responsibilities. As a writer, it seems to me, he was afraid most of all of being tedious and repetitious. And now he was glad because neither the theatre nor any editor's office could violate his tranquillity.

From CHEKHOV AND HIS RUSSIA

by W. H. Bruford

In his last and finest play, *The Cherry Orchard,* Chekhov returns to the theme of the land-owning class and its problems, but he presents their failure now not so much as a matter of personal or national character as of changing conditions of life. The play symbolises, poetically, yet without ever losing touch with reality, the transition from a purely agrarian to a more and more industrial Russia. It brings home to us the perplexity of the older generation of the aristocracy as the ground slips from under their feet, their attachment to the home and the way of life of their youth, with the sentiments of carefree ease and beauty associated with them in their minds, and their inability to master either their economic or their personal problems by resolutely facing facts. The central characters are the mondaine Liubov Andreyevna, the owner, with her brother Gaev, of an estate with a fine old cherry orchard, and Lopakhin, the merchant son of the village shopkeeper. We have come across him already as a representative of the peasant who has risen out of his class, in the new age of money, through his energy and business ability. Though he stands for another world, he is not hostile to Liubov. On the contrary, he remembers with gratitude her kindness to him as a boy. But the aristocrats, almost in spite of themselves, tend to look down on him, and his proposal for saving their estate, by letting the ground where the cherry orchard stands for building sites, fills them with horror. It is simply unthinkable, yet they see no other way out of their predicament. They watch their doom approaching with paralysed will, still vaguely hoping that somehow they will escape, and bring their ruin nearer all the time by the reckless extravagance to which they are accustomed.

Gaev, the brother, and his friend Simeonov-Pishchik, are merely background figures, not drawn in the round, but they suggest two types of decadent squire, the one seeking refuge from reality in fine words and sentiments, or solacing himself with billiards and lollypops, and the other, cruder, living on his friends, until minerals are found on his land by English prospectors. The Chekhov who wrote to Suvorin in 1891: 'Alas, I shall never be a Tolstoyan. In women I love beauty above all things; and in the history of mankind, culture, expressed in carpets, carriages with springs, and keenness of wit'— was drawn emotionally, one feels, to his aristocrats, as Goethe had been to his poet Tasso. But just as Goethe's wisdom had seen something right too in the prosaic Antonio, because even poets must have some regard for the society around them, so Chekhov would have the Russians realise that Lopakhin is a good fellow, and that what he represents is something to which Russia has to reconcile herself. For post-revolutionary critics he is even too kind to this bourgeois. He tries to marry him off with Varya, Liubov's adopted daughter, but there is always a hitch, perhaps because their classes are not quite ripe for fusion. And he holds out hope for the future in his picture of Liubov's young daughter, Anya, and the former tutor, Trofimov. Trofimov, the 'eternal student', the raisonneur of the piece, is given lines which express Chekhov's own thought as we know it from his letters, that men have little till now to be proud of; they should cease to be so pleased with themselves and simply work, as at present few do in Russia. Anya, under his influence, is ready to part from her dear cherry orchard. There will be still better places in the world that is yet to be. 'All Russia is our garden', Trofimov tells her, and the garden they are leaving is spoilt for them by the odour of serfdom which still clings to it. But this young man himself, who has not succeeded at thirty in taking a degree, is not a very promising leader towards the better world. As a representative of revolutionary youth he is not really convincing, and that not merely because of the caution imposed on any author by the censorship, say post-revolutionary critics. It may be, as they assume, because Chekhov was here drawing a type he did not know sufficiently well. Or it may be that he saw a good deal of the Ivanov even in Trofimov, and could not help treating him with a certain irony.

From THE IDEA OF A THEATRE

by Francis Fergusson

THE PLOT OF "THE CHERRY ORCHARD"

The Cherry Orchard is often accused of having no plot whatever, and it is true that the story gives little indication of the play's content or meaning; nothing happens, as the Broadway reviewers so often point out. Nor does it have a thesis, though many attempts have been made to attribute a thesis to it, to make it into a Marxian tract, or into a nostalgic defense of the old regime. The play does not have much of a plot in either of these accepted meanings of the word, for it is not addressed to the rationalizing mind but to the poetic and histrionic sensibility. It is an imitation of an action in the strictest sense, and it is plotted according to the first meaning of this word which I have distinguished in other contexts: the incidents are selected and arranged to define an action in a certain mode; a complete action, with a beginning, middle, and end in time. Its freedom from the mechanical order of the thesis or the intrigue is the sign of the perfection of Chekhov's realistic art. And its apparently casual incidents are actually composed with most elaborate and conscious skill to reveal the underlying life, and the natural, objective form of the play as a whole.

In *Ghosts,* as I showed, the action is distorted by the stereotyped requirements of the thesis and the intrigue.

That is partly a matter of the mode of action which Ibsen was trying to show; a quest "of ethical motivation" which requires some sort of intellectual framework, and yet can have no final meaning in the purely literal terms of Ibsen's theater. *The Cherry Orchard,* on the other hand, is a drama "of pathetic motivation," a theater-poem of the suffering of change; and this mode of action and awareness is much closer to the skeptical basis of modern realism, and to the histrionic basis of all realism. Direct perception before predication is always true, says Aristotle; and the extraordinary feat of Chekhov is to predicate nothing. This he achieves by means of his plot: he selects only those incidents, those moments in his characters' lives, between their rationalized efforts, when they sense their situation and destiny most directly. So he contrives to show the action of the play as a whole—the unsuccessful attempt to cling to the Cherry Orchard—in many diverse reflectors and without propounding any thesis about it.

The slight narrative thread which ties these incidents and characters together for the inquiring mind, is quickly recounted. The family that owns the old estate named after its famous orchard—Lyubov, her brother Gaev, and her daughters Varya and Anya—is all but bankrupt, and the question is how to prevent the bailiffs from selling the estate to pay their debts. Lopahin, whose family were formerly serfs on the estate, is now rapidly growing rich as a businessman, and he offers a very sensible plan: chop down the orchard, divide the property into small lots, and sell them off to make a residential suburb for the growing industrial town nearby. Thus the cash value of the estate could be not only preserved, but increased. But this would not save what Lyubov and her brother find valuable in the old estate; they cannot consent to the destruction of the orchard. But they cannot find, or earn, or borrow the money to pay their debts either; and in due course the estate is sold at auction to Lopahin himself, who will make a very good thing of it. His workmen are hacking at the old trees before the family is out of the house.

The play may be briefly described as a realistic ensemble pathos: the characters all suffer the passing of the estate in different ways, thus adumbrating this change at a deeper and more generally significant level than that of any individual's experience. The action which they all share by analogy, and which informs the suffering of the destined change of the Cherry Orchard, is "to save the Cherry Orchard": that is, each character sees some value in it—economic, sentimental, social, cultural—which he wishes to keep. By means of his plot, Chekhov always focuses attention on the general action: his crowded stage, full of the characters I have mentioned as well as half a dozen hangers-on, is like an implicit discussion of the fatality which concerns them all; but Chekhov does not believe in their ideas, and the interplay he shows among his *dramatis personae* is not so much the play of thought as the alternation of his characters' perceptions of their situation, as the moods shift and the time for decision comes and goes.

Though the action which Chekhov chooses to show on-stage is "pathetic," i.e., suffering and perception, it is complete: the Cherry Orchard is constituted before our eyes, and then dissolved. The first act is a prologue: it is the occasion of Lyubov's return from Paris to try to resume her old life. Through her eyes and those of her daughter Anya, as well as from the complementary perspectives of Lopahin and Trofimov, we see the estate as it were in the round, in its many possible meanings. The second act corresponds to the agon; it is in this act that we become aware of the conflicting values of all the characters, and of the efforts they make (off-stage) to save each one *his* Orchard. The third act corresponds to the pathos and peripety of the traditional tragic form. The occasion is a rather hysterical party which Lyubov gives while her estate is being sold at auction in the nearby town; it ends with Lopahin's announcement, in pride and the bitterness of guilt, that he was the purchaser. The last act is the epiphany: we see the action, now completed, in a new and ironic light. The occasion is the departure of the family: the windows are boarded up, the furniture piled in the corners, and the bags packed. All the characters feel, and the audience sees in a thousand ways, that the wish to save the Orchard has amounted in fact to destroying it; the gathering of its denizens to separation; the homecoming to departure. What this "means" we are not told. But the action is completed, and the poem of the suffering of change concludes in a new and final perception, and a rich chord of feeling.

The structure of each act is based upon a more or less ceremonious social occasion. In his use of the social ceremony—arrivals, departures, anniversaries, parties—Chekhov is akin to James. His purpose is the same: to focus attention on an action which all share by analogy, instead of upon the reasoned purpose of any individual, as Ibsen does in his drama of ethical motivation. Chekhov uses the social occasion also to reveal the individual at moments when he is least enclosed in his private rationalization and most open to disinterested insights. The Chekhovian ensembles may appear superficially to be mere pointless stalemates—too like family gatherings and arbitrary meetings which we know off-stage. So they are. But in his miraculous arrangement the very discomfort of many presences is made to reveal fundamental aspects of the human situation.

That Chekhov's art of plotting is extremely conscious and deliberate is clear the moment one considers the distinction between the stories of his characters as we learn about them, and the moments of their lives which he chose to show directly on-stage. Lopahin, for example, is a man of action like one of the new capitalists in Gorki's plays. Chekhov knew all about him, and could have shown us an exciting episode from his career if he had not chosen to see him only when he was forced to pause and pathetically sense his own motives in a wider context which qualifies their importance. Lyubov has been dragged about Europe for years by her ne'er-do-well lover, and her life might have yielded several sure-fire erotic intrigues like those of the commercial theater. But Chekhov, like all the great artists of modern times, rejected these standard motivations as both stale and false. The actress Arkadina, in *The Seagull,* remarks, as she closes a novel of Maupassant's, "Well, among the French that may be, but here with us there's nothing of the kind, we've no set program." In the context the irony of her remark is deep: she is herself a purest product of the commercial theater, and at that very time she is engaged in a love affair of the kind she objects to in Maupassant. But Chekhov, with his subtle art of plotting, has caught her in a situation, and at a brief moment of clarity and pause, when the falsity of her career is clear to all, even herself.

Thus Chekhov, by his art of plot-making, defines an action in the opposite mode to that of *Ghosts.* Ibsen defines a desperate quest for reasons and for ultimate, intelligible moral values. This action falls naturally into the form of the agon, and at the end of the play Ibsen is at a loss to develop the final pathos, or bring it to an end with an accepted perception. But the pathetic is the very mode of action and awareness which seems to Chekhov closest to the reality of the human situation, and by means of his plot he shows, even in characters who are not in themselves unusually passive, the suffering and the perception of change. The "moment" of human experience which *The Cherry Orchard* presents thus corresponds to that of the Sophoclean chorus, and of the evenings in the *Purgatorio. Ghosts* is a fighting play, armed for its sharp encounter with the rationalizing mind, its poetry concealed by its reasons. Chekhov's poetry, like Ibsen's, is behind the naturalistic surfaces; but the form of the play as a whole is "nothing but" poetry in the widest sense: the coherence of the concrete elements of the composition. Hence the curious vulnerability of Chekhov on the contemporary stage: he does not argue, he merely presents; and though his audiences even on Broadway are touched by the time they reach the last act, they are at a loss to say what it is all about.

It is this reticent objectivity of Chekhov also which makes him so difficult to analyze in words: he appeals exclusively to the histrionic sensibility where the little poetry of modern realism is to be found. Nevertheless, the effort of analysis must be made if one is to understand this art at all; and if the reader will bear with me, he is asked to consider one element, that of the scene, in the composition of the second act.

ACT II: THE SCENE AS A BASIC ELEMENT IN THE COMPOSITION

M. Cocteau writes, in his preface to *Les Mariés de la Tour Eiffel*: "The action of my play is in images (*imagée*) while the text is not: I attempt to substitute a 'poetry of the theater' for 'poetry in the theater.' Poetry in the theater is a piece of lace which it is impossible to see at a distance. Poetry of the theater would be coarse lace; a lace of ropes, a ship at sea. *Les Mariés* should have the frightening look of a drop of poetry under the microscope. The *scenes* are integrated like the *words* of a poem."

This description applies very exactly to *The Cherry Orchard*: the larger elements of the composition—the scenes or episodes, the setting and the developing story —are composed in such a way as to make a poetry of the theater; but the "text" as we read it literally, is not. Chekhov's method, as Mr. Stark Young puts it in the preface to his translation of *The Seagull*, "is to take actual material such as we find in life and manage it in such a way that the inner meanings are made to appear. On the surface the life in his plays is natural, possible, and at times in effect even casual."

Mr. Young's translations of Chekhov's plays, together with his beautifully accurate notes, explanations, and interpretations, have made the text of Chekhov at last available for the English-speaking stage, and for any reader who will bring to his reading a little patience and imagination.[1] Mr. Young shows us what Chekhov means in detail: by the particular words his characters use; by their rhythms of speech; by their gestures, pauses, and bits of stage business. In short, he makes the text transparent, enabling us to see through it to the music of action, the underlying poetry of the composition as a whole—and this is as much as to say that any study of Chekhov (lacking as we do adequate and available productions) must be based upon Mr. Young's work. At this point I propose to take this work for granted; to assume the translucent text; and to consider the role of the setting in the poetic or musical order of Act II.

The second act, as I have said, corresponds to the agon of the traditional plot scheme: it is here that we see most clearly the divisive purposes of the characters, the contrasts between their views of the Cherry Orchard itself. But the center of interest is not in these individual conflicts, nor in the contrasting visions for their own sake, but in the common fatality which they reveal: the passing of the old estate. The setting, as we come to know it behind the casual surfaces of the text, is one of the chief elements in this poem of change: if Act II were a lyric, instead of an act of a play, the setting would be a crucial word appearing in a succession of rich contexts which endow it with a developing meaning.

Chekhov describes the setting in the following realistic terms. "A field. An old chapel, long abandoned, with crooked walls, near it a well, big stones that apparently were once tombstones, and an old bench. A road to the estate of Gaev can be seen. On one side poplars rise, casting their shadows, the cherry orchard begins there. In the distance a row of telegraph poles; and far, far away, faintly traced on the horizon, is a large town, visible only in the clearest weather. The sun will soon be down."

To make this set out of a cyclorama, flats, cut-out silhouettes, and lighting-effects, would be difficult, without producing that unbelievable but literally intended —and in any case indigestible—scene which modern realism demands; and here Chekhov is uncomfortably bound by the convention of his time. The best strategy in production is that adopted by Robert Edmond Jones in his setting for *The Seagull*: to pay lip service only to the convention of photographic realism, and make the trees, the chapel and all the other elements as simple as possible. The less closely the setting is defined by the carpenter, the freer it is to play the role Chekhov wrote for it: a role which changes and develops in relation to the story. Shakespeare did not have this problem; he could present his setting in different ways at different moments in a few lines of verse:

> Alack! the night comes on, and the bleak winds
> Do sorely ruffle; for many miles about
> There's scarce a bush.

Chekhov, as we shall see, gives his setting life and flexibility in spite of the visible elements on-stage, not by means of the poetry of words but by means of his characters' changing sense of it.

When the curtain rises we see the setting simply as the country at the sentimental hour of sunset. Epihodov is playing his guitar and other hangers-on of the estate are loafing, as is their habit, before supper. The dialogue which starts after a brief pause focuses attention upon individuals in the group: Charlotta, the governess, boasting of her culture and complaining that no one understands her; the silly maid Dunyasha, who is infatuated with Yasha, Lyubov's valet. The scene, as reflected by these characters, is a satirical period-piece like the "Stag at Eve" or "The Maiden's Prayer"; and when the group falls silent and begins to drift away (having heard Lyubov, Gaev, and Lopahin approaching along the path) Chekhov expects us to smile at the sentimental clichés which the place and the hour have produced.

But Lyubov's party brings with it a very different atmosphere: of irritation, frustration, and fear. It is here we learn that Lopahin cannot persuade Lyubov and Gaev to put their affairs in order; that Gaev has been making futile gestures toward getting a job and borrowing money; that Lyubov is worried about the estate, about her daughters, and about her lover, who has now fallen ill in Paris. Lopahin, in a huff, offers to leave; but Lyubov will not let him go—"It's more cheerful with you here," she says; and this group in its turn falls silent. In the distance we hear the music of the Jewish orchestra—when Chekhov wishes us to raise our eyes from the people in the foreground to their wider setting, he often uses music as a signal and an inducement. This time the musical entrance of the setting into our consciousness is more urgent and sinister than it was before: we see not so much the peace of evening as the silhouette of the dynamic industrial town on the horizon, and the approach of darkness. After a little more desultory conversation, there is another pause, this time without music, and the foreboding aspect of the scene in silence is more intense.

In this silence Firs, the ancient servant, hurries on with Gaev's coat, to protect him from the evening chill, and we briefly see the scene through Firs's eyes. He remembers the estate before the emancipation of the serfs, when it was the scene of a way of life which made sense to him; and now we become aware of the frail relics of this life: the old gravestones and the chapel "fallen out of the perpendicular."

In sharpest contrast with this vision come the young voices of Anya, Varya, and Trofimov who are approaching along the path. The middle-aged and the old in the foreground are pathetically grateful for this note of youth, of strength, and of hope; and presently they are listening happily (though without agreement or belief) to Trofimov's aspirations, his creed of social progress, and his conviction that their generation is no longer important to the life of Russia. When the group falls silent again, they are all disposed to contentment with the moment; and when Epihodov's guitar is heard, and we look up, we feel the country and the evening under the aspect of hope—as offering freedom from the responsibilities and conflicts of the estate itself:

(EPIHODOV *passes by at the back, playing his guitar.*)

Lyubov.
(*Lost in thought.*) Epihodov is coming—
Anya.
(*Lost in thought.*) Epihodov is coming.
Gaev.
The sun has set, ladies and gentlemen.
Trofimov.
Yes.
Gaev.
(*Not loud and as if he were declaiming.*) Oh, Nature, wonderful, you gleam with eternal radiance, beautiful and indifferent, you, whom we call Mother, combine in yourself both life and death, you give life and take it away.
Varya.
(*Beseechingly.*) Uncle!

Gaev's false, rhetorical note ends the harmony, brings us back to the present and to the awareness of change on the horizon, and produces a sort of empty stalemate —a silent pause with worry and fear in it.

(*All sit absorbed in their thoughts. There is only the silence.* FIRS *is heard muttering to himself softly. Suddenly a distant sound is heard, as if from the sky, like the sound of a snapped string, dying away, mournful.*)

This mysterious sound is used like Epihodov's strumming to remind us of the wider scene, but (though distant) it is sharp, almost a warning signal, and all the characters listen and peer toward the dim edges of the horizon. In their attitudes and guesses Chekhov reflects, in rapid succession, the contradictory aspects of the scene which have been developed at more length before us:

Lyubov.
What's that?
Lopahin.
I don't know. Somewhere far off in a mine shaft a bucket fell. But somewhere very far off.
Gaev.
And it may be some bird—like a heron.
Trofimov.
Or an owl—
Lyubov.
(*Shivering.*) It's unpleasant, somehow. (*A pause.*)
Firs.
Before the disaster it was like that. The owl hooted and the samovar hummed without stopping, both.
Gaev.
Before what disaster?
Firs.
Before the emancipation.

(*A pause.*)

Lyubov.
You know, my friends, let's go. . . .

Lyubov feels the need to retreat, but the retreat is turned into flight when "the wayfarer" suddenly appears on the path asking for money. Lyubov in her bewilderment, her sympathy, and her bad conscience, gives him gold. The party breaks up, each in his own way thwarted and demoralized.

Anya and Trofimov are left on-stage; and, to conclude his theatrical poem of the suffering of change, Chekhov reflects the setting in them:

Anya.

(*A pause.*) It's wonderful here today!

Trofimov.

Yes, the weather is marvelous.

Anya.

What have you done to me, Petya, why don't I love the cherry orchard any longer the way I used to? I loved it too tenderly; it seemed to me there was not a better place on earth than our orchard.

Trofimov.

All Russia is our garden. The earth is immense and beautiful. . . .

The sun has set, the moon is rising with its chill and its ancient animal excitement, and the estate is dissolved in the darkness as Nineveh is dissolved in a pile of rubble with vegetation creeping over it. Chekhov wishes to show the Cherry Orchard as "gone"; but for this purpose he employs not only the literal time-scheme (sunset to moonrise) but, as reflectors, Anya and Trofimov, for whom the present in any form is already gone and only the bodiless future is real. Anya's young love for Trofimov's intellectual enthusiasm (like Juliet's "all as boundless as the sea") has freed her from her actual childhood home, made her feel "at home in the world" anywhere. Trofimov's abstract aspirations give him a chillier and more artificial, but equally complete, detachment not only from the estate itself (he disapproves of it on theoretical grounds) but from Anya (he thinks it would be vulgar to be in love with her). We hear the worried Varya calling for Anya in the distance; Anya and Trofimov run down to the river to discuss the socialistic *Paradiso Terrestre;* and with these complementary images of the human scene, and this subtle chord of feeling, Chekhov ends the act.

The "scene" is only one element in the composition of Act II, but it illustrates the nature of Chekhov's poetry of the theater. It is very clear, I think, that Chekhov is not trying to present us with a rationalization of social change *à la* Marx, or even with a subtler rationalization

à la Shaw. On the other hand, he is not seeking, like
Wagner, to seduce us into one passion. He shows us
a moment of change in society, and he shows us a
"pathos"; but the elements of his composition are always taken as objectively real. He offers us various
rationalizations, various images and various feelings,
which cannot be reduced either to one emotion or to
one idea: they indicate an action and a scene which is
"there" before the rational formulations, or the emotionally charged attitudes, of any of the characters.

The surrounding scene of *The Cherry Orchard* corresponds to the significant stage of human life which
Sophocles' choruses reveal, and to the empty wilderness
beyond Ibsen's little parlor. We miss, in Chekhov's
scene, any fixed points of human significance, and that
is why, compared with Sophocles, he seems limited and
partial—a bit too pathetic even for our bewildered
times. But, precisely because he subtly and elaborately
develops the moments of pathos with their sad insights,
he sees much more in the little scene of modern realism
than Ibsen does. Ibsen's snowpeaks strike us as rather
hysterical; but the "stage of Europe" which we divine
behind the Cherry Orchard is confirmed by a thousand
impressions derived from other sources. We may recognize its main elements in a cocktail party in Connecticut
or Westchester: someone's lawn full of voluble people;
a dry white clapboard church (instead of an Orthodox
chapel) just visible across a field; time passing, and the
muffled roar of a four-lane highway under the hill—or
we may be reminded of it in the final section of *The
Wasteland,* with its twittering voices, its old gravestones
and deserted chapel, and its dim crowd on the horizon
foreboding change. It is because Chekhov says so little
that he reveals so much, providing a concrete basis for
many conflicting rationalizations of contemporary social
change: by accepting the immediacy and unintelligibility
of modern realism so completely, he in some ways
transcends its limitations, and prepares the way for
subsequent developments in the modern theater.

Chekhov's Histrionic Art:
An End and a Beginning

> Era già l'ora che volge il disio
> ai naviganti, e intenercisce il core
> lo dì ch'han detto ai dolci amici addio;
> e che lo nuovo peregrin d'amore
> punge, se ode squilla di lontano,
> che paia il giorno pianger che si more.
> —*Purgatorio*, CANTO VIII[1]

The poetry of modern realistic drama is to be found in those inarticulate moments when the human creature is shown responding directly to his immediate situation. Such are the many moments—composed, interrelated, echoing each other—when the waiting and loafing characters in Act II get a fresh sense (one after the other, and each in his own way) of their situation on the doomed estate. It is because of the exactitude with which Chekhov perceives and imitates these tiny responses, that he can make them echo each other, and convey, when taken together, a single action with the scope, the general significance or suggestiveness, of poetry. Chekhov, like other great dramatists, has what might be called an ear for action, comparable to the trained musician's ear for musical sound.

The action which Chekhov thus imitates in his second act (that of lending ear, in a moment of freedom from practical pressures, to impending change) echoes, in its turn, a number of other poets: Laforgue's "poetry of waiting-rooms" comes to mind, as well as other works stemming from the period of hush before the first World War. The poets are to some extent talking about the same thing, and their works, like voices in a continuing colloquy, help to explain each other: hence the justification and the purpose of seeking comparisons. The eighth

[1] It was now the hour that turns back the desire of those who sail the seas and melts their heart, that day when they have said to their sweet friends adieu, and that pierces the new pilgrim with love, if from afar he hears the chimes which seem to mourn for the dying day.

canto of the *Purgatorio* is widely separated from *The Cherry Orchard* in space and time, but these two poems unmistakably echo and confirm each other. Thinking of them together, one can begin to place Chekhov's curiously non-verbal dramaturgy and understand the purpose and the value of his reduction of the art to histrionic terms, as well as the more obvious limitations which he thereby accepts. For Dante accepts similar limitations at this point but locates the mode of action he shows here at a certain point in his vast scheme.

The explicit co-ordinates whereby Dante places the action of Canto VIII might alone suffice to give one a clue to the comparison with *The Cherry Orchard:* we are in the Valley of Negligent Rulers who, lacking light, unwillingly suffer their irresponsibility, just as Lyubov and Gaev do. The ante-purgatorio is behind us, and purgatory proper, with its hoped-for work, thought, and moral effort, is somewhere ahead, beyond the night which is now approaching. It is the end of the day; and as we wait, watch, and listen, evening moves slowly over our heads, from sunset to darkness to moonrise. Looking more closely at this canto, one can see that Dante the Pilgrim, and the Negligent Rulers he meets, are listening and looking as Chekhov's characters are in Act II: the action is the same; in both a childish and uninstructed responsiveness, an unpremeditated obedience to what is actual, informs the suffering of change. Dante the author, for his elaborate and completely conscious reasons, works here with the primitive histrionic sensibility, he composes with elements sensuously or sympathetically, but not rationally or verbally, defined. The rhythms, the pauses, and the sound effects he employs are strikingly similar to Chekhov's. And so he shows himself—Dante "the new Pilgrim"—meeting this mode of awareness for the first time: as delicately and ignorantly as Gaev when he feels all of a sudden the extent of evening, and before he falsifies his perception with his embarrassing apostrophe to Nature.

If Dante allows himself as artist and as protagonist

only the primitive sensibility of the child, the naïf, the natural saint, at this point in the ascent, it is because, like Chekhov, he is presenting a threshold or moment of change in human experience. He wants to show the unbounded potentialities of the psyche before or between the moments when it is morally and intellectually realized. In Canto VIII the pilgrim is both a child, and a child who is changing; later moments of transition are different. Here he is virtually (but for the Grace of God) lost; all the dangers are present. Yet he remains uncommitted and therefore open to finding himself again and more truly. In all of this the parallel to Chekhov is close. But because Dante sees this moment as a moment only in the ascent, Canto VIII is also composed in ways in which Act II of *The Cherry Orchard* is not—ways which the reader of the *Purgatorio* will not understand until he looks back from the top of the mountain. Then he will see the homesickness which informs Canto VIII in a new light, and all of the concrete elements, the snake in the grass, the winged figures that roost at the edge of the valley like night-hawks, will be intelligible to the mind and, without losing their concreteness, take their places in a more general frame. Dante's fiction is laid in the scene beyond the grave, where every human action has its relation to ultimate reality, even though that relation becomes explicit only gradually. But Chekhov's characters are seen in the flesh and in their very secular emotional entanglements: in the contemporary world as anyone can see it—nothing visible beyond the earth's horizon, with its signs of social change. The fatality of the *Zeitgeist* is the ultimate reality in the theater of modern realism; the anagoge is lacking. And though Ibsen and Chekhov are aware of both history and moral effort, they do not know what to make of them—perhaps they reveal only illusory perspectives, "masquerades which time resumes." If Chekhov echoes Dante, it is not because of what he ultimately understood but because of the accuracy with which he saw and imitated that moment of action.

If one thinks of the generation to which Anya and Trofimov were supposed to belong, it is clear that the new motives and reasons which they were to find, after their inspired evening together, were not such as to turn all Russia, or all the world, into a garden. The potentialities which Chekhov presented at that moment of change were not to be realized in the wars and revolutions which followed: what actually followed was rather that separation and destruction, that scattering and destinationless trekking, which he also sensed as possible. But, in the cultivation of the dramatic art after Chekhov, renewals, the realization of hidden potentialities, did follow. In Chekhov's histrionic art, the "desire is turned back" to its very root, to the immediate response, to the movements of the psyche before they are limited, defined, and realized in reasoned purpose. Thus Chekhov revealed hidden potentialities, if not in the life of the time, at least in ways of seeing and showing human life; if not in society, at least in the dramatic art. The first and most generally recognized result of these labors was to bring modern realism to its final perfection in the productions of the Moscow Art Theater and in those who learned from it. But the end of modern realism was also a return to very ancient sources; and in our time the fertilizing effect of Chekhov's humble objectivity may be traced in a number of dramatic forms which cannot be called modern realism at all.

The acting technique of the Moscow Art Theater is so closely connected, in its final development, with Chekhov's dramaturgy, that it would be hard to say which gave the more important clues. Stanislavsky and Nemirovitch-Danchenko from one point of view, and Chekhov from another, approached the same conception: both were searching for an attitude and a method that would be less hidebound, truer to experience, than the cliché–responses of the commercial theater. The Moscow Art Theater taught the performer to make that direct and total response which is the root of poetry in the widest sense: they cultivated the histrionic sensibility

in order to free the actor to realize, in his art, the situa-
tions and actions which the playwright had imagined.
Chekhov's plays demand this accuracy and imaginative
freedom from the performer; and the Moscow Art
Theater's productions of his works were a demonstration of the perfection, the reticent poetry, of modern
realism. And modern realism of this kind is still alive
in the work of many artists who have been more or
less directly influenced either by Chekhov or by the
Moscow Art Theater. In our country, for instance, there
is Clifford Odets; in France, Vildrac and Bernard, and
the realistic cinema, of which *Symphonie Pastorale* is
a recent example.

But this cultivation of the histrionic sensibility, bringing modern realism to its end and its perfection, also
provided fresh access to many other dramatic forms.
The Moscow technique, when properly developed and
critically understood, enables the producer and performer to find the life in any theatrical form; and before
the revolution the Moscow Art Theater had thus re-
vivified *Hamlet, Carmen,* the interludes of Cervantes,
Neoclassic comedies of several kinds, and many other
works which were not realistic in the modern sense at
all. A closely related acting technique underlay Rein-
hardt's virtuosity; and Copeau, in the Vieux Colombier,
used it to renew not only the art of acting but, by that
means, the art of play-writing also. I shall return to
this development in the last chapter, when I discuss
Obey's *Noah,* a play based upon Chekhovian modes of
awareness but transcending the limitations of modern
realism by means of the Biblical legend.

After periods when great drama is written, great per-
formers usually appear to carry on the life of the theater
for a few more generations. Such were the Siddonses
and Macreadys who kept the great Shakespearian roles
alive after Shakespeare's theater was gone, and such, at
a further stage of degeneration, were the mimes of the
Commedia dell'Arte, improvising on the themes of
Terence and Plautus when the theater had lost most of

its meaning. The progress of modern realism from Ibsen to Chekhov looks in some respects like a withering and degeneration of this kind: Chekhov does not demand the intellectual scope, the ultimate meanings, which Ibsen demanded, and to some critics Chekhov does not look like a real dramatist but merely an over-developed mime, a stage virtuoso. But the theater of modern realism did not afford what Ibsen demanded, and Chekhov is much the more perfect master of its little scene. If Chekhov drastically reduced the dramatic art, he did so in full consciousness, and in obedience both to artistic scruples and to a strict sense of reality. He reduced the dramatic art to its ancient root, from which new growths are possible.

But the tradition of modern realism is not the only version of the theater in our time. The stage itself, belying the realistic pretense of artlessness and pseudo-scientific truth, is there. Most of the best contemporary play-writing accepts the stage "as stage," and by so doing tries to escape realistic limitations altogether. In the following chapters I propose to sample this effort in several kinds of modern plays.

From CURTAINS

by Kenneth Tynan

The Cherry Orchard, by Anton Chekhov, at Sadler's Wells, London.

The great thing about the Moscow Art Theatre's production of *The Cherry Orchard* is that it blows the cobwebs off the play. And who put them there? Why, we ourselves. We have remade Chekhov's last play in our image just as drastically as the Germans have remade *Hamlet* in theirs. Our *Cherry Orchard* is a pathetic symphony, to be played in a mood of elegy. We invest it with a nostalgia for the past which, though it runs right through our culture, is alien to Chekhov's. His people are country gentry: we make them into decadent aristocrats.

Next, we romanticise them. Their silliness becomes pitiable grotesquerie; and at this point our hearts warm to them. They are not Russians at all: they belong in the great line of English eccentrics. The upstart Lopakhin, who buys up their heritage, cannot be other than a barbarous bounder. Having foisted on Chekhov a collection of patrician mental cases, we then congratulate him on having achieved honorary English citizenship. Meanwhile the calm, genial sanity of the play has flown out of the window. In M. Stanitsyn's production it is magnificently restored. Common-sense is not a quality we like to attribute to our artists; we prefer them slightly deranged; but Chekhov had it in full measure, and so have his present, peerless interpreters. Did I say this was Chekhov without the cobwebs? It is more: it is a total spring-cleaning.

Part of its freshness comes from the fact that it is a brand-new production, with new décor and several newly graduated players: on this tour the Art Theatre is clearly experimenting with youth. But there is more to it than that. The real novelty lies in its attitude towards Mme. Ranevsky's feckless household. This is not the old régime, crazily expiring with a pathetic jest on its lips. It is a real family, capricious perhaps and irresponsible, but essentially normal and undoomed. The play becomes what Chekhov called it: a comedy. "In places, even a farce," he added, but M. Stanitsyn does not go as far as that. He simply treats the characters as recognisable human beings in a mess, rather than as freaks trapped in a tragic *impasse*.

M. Massalsky's Gayev, for example, is no crumbling dodderer but the man of "suavity and elegance" whom Chekhov imagined: the decay is internal and moral. Nor is there anything of the neurotic spinster in Mlle. Lennikova's Varya: she is a practical, good-hearted girl who blushes too much to be easily marriageable; and her collapse, when Lopakhin lets her down, is the more moving for its lack of neurotic preparation. Lopakhin himself behaves, as Chekhov demanded, "with the utmost courtesy and decorum": no thrusting vulgarity here, but a mature impatience which rises, in the third-act announcement that he is the master now, to an astonishing climax of dismayed exasperation. The actor, M. Lukyanov, plays like a master throughout.

One crucial test remains: what does the production invite us to make of Trofimov, the eternal student with his vision of a transformed Russia? The English habit is to present him as a hare-brained booby whom no one could possibly take seriously. Yet the Czarist censor took him seriously enough to expunge several of his more critical speeches. M. Gubanov's performance is delicately right: a bundle of nerves, forever fingering his spectacles, and a fumbler in matters of emotion, but intelligent and sincere withal—a true misfit, but also a true prophet. This is straight Chekhov, not propagandist distortion. It is we who, by turning the other members of Ranevsky's household into caricatures of highborn futility, have infected the text with unnecessary social significance.

There are many more actors to salute—it is in the nature of this glowing troupe that it bats all the way down the list. I think of M. Leonidov's Yasha, more cad's cad than gent's gent, embracing the maid Dunyasha and blowing cigar-smoke into her eyes as she smiles at him. Of M. Yanshin's earth-larding Pischchik, frantically feeling for his purse after the conjuring tricks have been played. Of M. Kornukov's plump Epikhodov, pocketing an apple to make up for his rejection by Dunyasha. And I have not yet mentioned Alexis Gribov, one of the great actors of the world, who plays the tiny part of Firs, the ancient butler—fixed like a statue, in jaundiced petrifaction, and held upright only by handy walking-sticks or tables. Are there no weaknesses? For me, yes: I thought Mme. Tarassova inexpressive and unmoving. This is not a failure of conception; Chekhov expressly forbade the romantic agonies which most actresses bring to Mme. Ranevsky. It is a failure of execution. The actress is simply monotonous.

SELECTED BIBLIOGRAPHY

Bruford, W. H., *Chekhov*, London, 1957.

_____*Chekhov and His Russia: A Sociological Study*, London, 1947.

Brustein, Robert, *The Theatre of Revolt*, Boston, 1964.

Chekhov, A. P., *Letters to O. L. Knipper*, translated by Constance Garnett, London, 1926.

_____*Letters on the Short Story, the Drama, and Other Literary Topics*, edited by Louis S. Friedland, London, 1924.

_____*Notebooks*, translated by S. S. Koteliansky and Leonard Woolf, London, 1921.

_____*Selected Letters*, edited by Lillian Hellman and translated by Sidonie Lederer, New York, 1955.

Gerhardi, William, *Anton Chehov: A Critical Study*, London, 1923.

Gorky, Maxim, *Reminiscences of Tolstoy, Chekhov and Andreyev*, London, 1934.

Hingley, Ronald, *Chekhov*, London, 1950.

Katzer, Julius, ed., *A. P. Chekhov 1860-1960*, Moscow, 1960.

Koteliansky, S. S., ed., *Anton Tchekhov: Literary and Theatrical Reminiscences*, London, 1927.

_____and P. Tomlinson, *Life and Letters of Anton Tchekhov*, London, 1925.

Kronenberger, Louis, *The Republic of Letters*, New York, 1955.

Magarshack, David, *Chekhov: A Life*, New York, 1953.

_____*Chekhov the Dramatist*, London, 1952.

Mann, Thomas, *Last Essays*, New York, 1959.

Muchnic, Helen, *An Introduction to Russian Literature*, New York, 1947.

Nemirovich-Danchenko, Vladimir, *My Life in the Russian Theatre*, Boston, 1937.

Peacock, Ronald, *The Poet in the Theatre*, London, 1946.

Simmons, Ernest J., *Chekhov*, Boston, 1962.

Stanislavsky, Constantin, *My Life in Art*, Boston, 1924.

Toumanova, Princess Nina Andronikova, *Anton Chekhov: The Voice of Twilight Russia*, New York, 1937.

Williams, Raymond, *Drama from Ibsen to Eliot*, London, 1952.

Yermilov, Vladimir, *A. P. Chekhov*, Moscow, n. d.

RECORDING: In Russian, with the Moscow Art Theatre: Bruno Hi-Fi Records 23020-2. (3 records)